Congregational Trauma:

Caring, Coping & Learning

Jill M. Hudson

An Alban Institute Publication

Library of Congress Catalog Card Number 98-73668
ISBN 1-56699-205-2

CONTENTS

ACKNOWLEDGMENTS

I am grateful to many people for sharing their stories of faith and courage, for directing me to resources, and for praying for me during the writing of this book. Each of them hopes that his or her experience of pain and loss can help others who may face a similar challenge. I also express appreciation to the Presbytery of Whitewater Valley of the Presbyterian Church (U.S.A.), which allowed me to use my educational leave for writing this book.

Special gratitude is extended to my friend, the poet and author Margaret Anne Huffman, and to Judson Press for permission to begin each chapter with a quotation from *"Through the Valley. . ." Prayers for Violent Times* (Valley Forge, Pa.: Judson Press, 1996).

The heart and soul of this work come from the tears and faithful service of many individuals who were personally involved in traumatic situations. I have listed them in the context of experience and contributions.

I would like to thank the Rev. Donna Wells, the Rev. Jerry Weber, the Rev. Donald Durrett, the Rev. Ronald Smith, the Rev. Carol McDonald, Kimberly Koczan, Ruth Moore, and Mark Moore from Northminster Presbyterian Church, Indianapolis.

I would like to thank Carol Travelstead, Capt. Mark Mason, the Rev. Wally Jeffs, the Rev. Tom Bartley, the Rev. Riley Walker, and the Rev. John Parsley for their assistance in writing the case study of First Baptist Church, Shelbyville, Indiana.

I would like to thank all the people who reflected with me on the trauma resulting from the bombing of the Alfred P. Murrah Federal Building, with particular appreciation to the Rev. Guy Ames and the Rev. Boyce Bowden for hosting my visit to Oklahoma City and suggesting individuals with whom I could speak. Participating in interviews were the Rev. Margaret Ball, the Rev. LeRoy Thompson, the Rev. Michael Fletcher-Taylor, the Rev. Gale Izard, the Rev. John Rusco, the Rev. Steve Vinson, the Rev. David Poteet, the Rev. Delbert Hamm, the Rev. Dene Brown, the Rev. Tracey Evans, the Rev. Rita Cowan, the Rev. Guy Ames, and P. G. Legg.

My thanks also to Dr. Kay Schrader of St. Vincent Stress Centers for providing materials from the Indianapolis School Crisis Response Team, as well as her insights gleaned from many years as a therapist and trainer. The Rev. William Weber was helpful in providing materials on the spiritual and emotional issues in post-trauma treatment.

Judith Cebula and Rich Van Wyck were of invaluable assistance in understanding the tasks and functioning of the media in times of crisis.

I would like to thank Dr. Edgar Towne, Dr. Rebecca Pritchard, and the Rev. Stanley Hankins for their critique of the manuscript. The Rev. Raymond Marquette receives my highest praise for his truly remarkable computer assistance. Julia Hickman, my administrative assistant, and Jo-Ann Young spent hours on this manuscript and are deserving of thanks. The red pen of Beth Ann Gaede, my editor, was very helpful!

The encouragement of my husband, Jay, remains at the heart of any creative endeavor I undertake. His presence during my personal times of trauma remains a gift from God. I am particularly grateful to him for encouraging me to put into print what I have learned from helping churches cope with trauma.

This book is dedicated in loving memory to the Rev. C. Frederick Mathias and his wife, Cleta. I miss them dearly.

INTRODUCTION

Murder. Arson. Bombings. Airline crashes. Pedophilia. Suicide. Newspaper exposés. Lover's revenge. Do these sound like the topics of a *New York Times* best-seller list? Yes, but they are also real-life happenings that touched the church of Jesus Christ over the past three years. I refer not to individuals in particular congregations who were affected by such atrocious acts, but to entire communities of faith that were directly struck by events we would label traumatic. These tragedies did not necessarily happen in Los Angeles or New York; most occurred in the sleepy Midwestern state of Indiana and touched the ministries of Presbyterian, American Baptist, Christian Church (Disciples of Christ), and Roman Catholic congregations. Trauma can strike anywhere, anytime, and the church is generally ill prepared to respond.

I learned this sobering truth firsthand when the presbytery I serve was faced with unbelievable horror—the brutal murder of a beloved pastor and his wife in their home ten days before Christmas 1996. After the first week of crisis, I turned to my library for resources and guidance. Although there were excellent resources available from a mental-health perspective, I could not find one book that addressed all the issues of trauma that could help a community of faith in response and recovery.

Ron Taylor, headmaster of the school in Dunblane, Scotland, where a man slaughtered 16 five- and six-year-old students and their teachers in March 1996, summed up the craziness of our world: "Evil visited us yesterday, and we don't know why." These extremely violent occurrences are becoming more and more a part of life. "Big World, Small Screen," a report of the American Psychological Association, informs us that the average child completing elementary school will have witnessed at least 8,000 murders and more than 100,000 other acts of assorted violence on television.

It is a shock but should be no surprise when an 11-year-old and a 13-year-old are arrested in Jonesboro, Arkansas, for opening fire on classmates and teachers at their middle school. Hate crimes, both racially motivated and against society at large, are on the rise. The bombings of the World Trade Center in New York City and the Alfred P. Murrah Federal Building in Oklahoma City have shattered our self-image of invincibility to terrorism. Sexual violence against children, women, and homosexuals continues to dominate our headlines. We are a nation seeking a quick fix with little indication that the underlying causes for the malaise in our country are being addressed. How can the church cope with such a world? Where is the Gospel for us when we're on the receiving end of these scenarios?

This book does not provide all the answers, but I hope that it will be a start. My eventual hope is that it will gather dust as it sits unneeded on shelves. The response to my call for case studies in the Alban Institute journal *Congregations* suggests, however, that such will not be the case. I fear that our trials and tribulations with this world of violence are not yet over. I hope readers will find this book before they need it.

Chapter 1 examines the theological and faith issues arising out of tragedy. Chapter 2 distinguishes between "crisis" and "trauma" and discusses grief and healing. Chapter 3 tells stories of congregations struggling amid brokenness and provides a case background for further reflection. Chapter 4 is designed to address the needs and resources for both natural disasters and those caused by human hands. Strategies for congregational care, with emphasis on various groups within the church, can be found in Chapter 5. Chapter 6 looks at the power of public worship in the healing of the congregation and examines occasions for worship in the progress of healing. Methods for dealing with newspapers, television crews, law-enforcement personnel, and trials are discussed in Chapter 7. Chapter 8 speaks to those who seek to care for the congregation from outside its membership and identifies the important role of judicatory officials. Chapter 9 closes with a look toward the future and identifies signs of healing.

I offer this work as a beginning guide for pastors, congregational leaders, judicatory executives, and others who are potential caregivers to churches in times of trauma. May God bless each of them in ministering to the wounded, angry, and brokenhearted.

CHAPTER 1

A Question of Faith: Why?

We need answers. If you are going to help us to recover, we can't believe you would send violence, let it happen, watch, evaluate our responses, and turn coldly away. You cannot dispense violation and healing at the same time and still be a God we trust to heal. You cannot be a double-minded, two-faced parent. What, O God, are we to do with you?

—Margaret Anne Huffman,
"Through the Valley..." Prayers for Violent Times, p. 168

When Rabbi Harold Kushner wrote *When Bad Things Happen to Good People* in 1981, he knew it might fill a need for people of faith. What he didn't anticipate was just how large an impact his book would have on the Jewish and Christian communities. All over America and throughout the world, people longing for answers about the nature of God and the nature of suffering gathered in church-school classes, in synagogue discussion groups, and around dining-room tables to talk about this little book. It was probably the most frequently used nonscriptural text for preaching over the next several years.

Why this unprecedented response? Because we want to know. We want to know and believe that God is, in fact, in charge of this crazy world. If God is at the helm, then how could such terrible tragedies—the Holocaust, murder, child abuse—how could these things happen in the world of an all-loving God? It is an inevitable question, one that we can explore but perhaps never fully answer.

One primary task of recovering from trauma for the religious person is the eventual integration of the absurd reality of what has happened into one's understanding of life. Even mature Christians find that faith may be shaken while trust in God remains. In the wake of trauma, there appears always to be some period, whether intense or mild, of questioning life's meaning and purpose and wondering if the God in whom we've believed has an active role in the world. In the wonderful book *All Our Losses, All Our Griefs,* pastoral counselors Kenneth Mitchell and Herbert Anderson point out that the life of faith is an ongoing task of building and rebuilding. Questioning is the start of the rebuilding phase for most people, and we need to assure each other that God *is* able to handle our doubts and questions.[1] Perhaps God even welcomes them.

Different Talk for Different Walks

"God was with me, my life was spared, and I feel I am blessed."

"God saved my life for a reason. There must be something God still wants me to do."

"I didn't choose the seat I had, but I accepted it as from the Lord. Those of us in that row were the only ones who survived. Maybe God was trying to tell me something."

"This trip was a last-minute decision. I wasn't sure I wanted to go, but things worked out so smoothly—and now this. Was it really what God wanted me to do?"

These four possible responses of survivors after a fatal plane crash illustrate different ways that people use "God-talk."[2] In an article on trauma and suffering, Dr. Anne Sutherland reminds us that all of these responses are patterns found in the Bible. The ideas that we are God's "chosen" people, that God makes things happen for a reason, that context can influence events, and that life is a complicated pattern of growth and change influenced by many interacting factors—all these are found in the stories of God's people struggling to understand life. Dr. Sutherland's research suggests that many people shift their primary mode, or "world-frame," when trauma or suffering strikes. Many times people revert to the comfort of patterns learned in childhood or early in their faith development.[3] As a pastor, I have observed this phenomenon when generally thoughtful and logical people utter such remarks as "It was God's will" or "Perhaps God needed another angel for the choir" upon the untimely death of a young child. Removed from the situation, such comments might seem outrageous, even to the person who has just uttered them. In their desperate attempt to comfort, people often regress to a more simplistic understanding of their faith.

One of the most serious difficulties in communications faced by pastors or caregivers is the discovery that the suffering person uses God-talk in a form different from that of the minister or comforter. A person's theology is always expressed through the culture in which he or she lives or was reared. It is important for us to be sensitive to the theological framework expressed. In trying times, most people need comfort, not a theological discussion. We should note that people need to have already developed an adequate theology and language to express it, without the need for teaching at the moment of trauma.[4] The fact that people struggle with language to express their beliefs reflects an inadequacy in articulating a theology of suffering.

Rather than critique or judge the maturity of a person's faith, the pastor or caregiver should recognize the limitations of language in expressing what we believe at times such as these. The stress and sorrow of the moment frequently lead to emotional responses that desperately seek comfort in our earliest roots rather than our matured faith. These are moments for listening and loving, not for teaching, correcting, or even answering. Most people who are suffering would be unable to accept our answers anyway.[5]

We should also be aware that when the forces of trauma overwhelm us, the concept of God with which we start may not match the understanding of God we hold when the trauma is over. Our relationship with God and our experience of God are no longer storybook-perfect. Something has happened that we cannot fit into our view of the Christian experience. Suddenly God is no longer the God who "keeps us from all harm" but a God whose role is quickly changing. Like Job, we suspect that we will know more about God at the end of this ordeal than at the beginning.

Where Has God Gone?

In times of loss, God may seem very far away. Our beliefs about God seem as unstable as a house of cards. The purpose of this chapter is not to provide an in-depth theological examination of the nature of good and evil. It is, however, to point the reader toward resources and schools of thought that may bring comfort and help in the powerful reshaping of beliefs that so often occurs during and after tragic loss. Ultimately, in the midst of trauma, questions arise: Who's in charge here? Why did this happen? Can this God of ours really overcome the power of darkness?

The theological pursuit of these questions is at the heart of the study of *theodicy*. Theodicy struggles to understand how a loving God could allow evil to exist. It is always a temptation to turn to Scripture for pat answers. Biblical answers are not, however, always entirely satisfying. The questions raised during times of trauma are so complex that even a thoughtful reading of Scripture can leave us with questions. For instance, Psalm 32:3-5 declares that illness results from sin, and that therefore the one who is silent and unwilling to confess continues to suffer. When, however, one says, "I will confess my transgressions to the Lord," one is forgiven and healed. It is only a short step to assuming that tragedy results solely from sin. This belief seems irreconcilable with Jesus' words about the man born blind: "Neither this man nor his parents sinned" (John 9:3). Or consider 1 Peter 1:6-7, where it is suggested that suffering tests the genuineness of faith and produces a witness to Christ's glory. Are we to understand tragedy as some sort of "test" that God inflicts on us? Not according to James 1:13: "No one, when tempted, should say, 'I am being tempted by God'; for God cannot be tempted by evil and he himself tempts no one." This is not to say that the Scriptures cannot help us understand our faith, but rather that we need to add theological reflection and prayer to the mix to talk about, if not resolve, our tensions when we face the mystery of tragedy.

I will briefly consider how we must place our trust in the sovereign reign of God, the role of lament as a valid response to God, the struggle to understand evil and suffering, and the nature of forgiveness. The reader can find more thorough treatments of these subjects in a theological resource.

When Abraham asks, "Shall not the Judge of all the earth do what is just?" (Gen. 18:25), he expresses for all of us our trust that God will be fair. But the notion of a fair God *and* an all-powerful God gives Rabbi Kushner difficulty. Kushner does not believe that God causes or prevents all our misfortunes. Some are caused by bad people, or bad luck, or the world of inflexible natural laws in which we live. For him God is neither perfect nor all-powerful. Instead, God remains with us, suffers with us, and offers support. Kushner holds that God *cannot* keep trauma from happening. God created a world in which more good happens than bad. This insight, unfortunately, is hard for most of us to remember in the midst of tragedy. Only time and distance help us to put the good and the bad in perspective. The facts of life or death are neutral. Our *response* to these facts is what gives them a positive or negative meaning. It is our job to interpret death to the living.[6] This perspective is difficult for denominations of the Reformed tradition and for many evangelical Christians who believe that God is always in control. However, we should not totally dismiss this viewpoint. The way we cope with death and the way we speak of God's victory over death are critically important in sharing our faith perspectives.

The Challenge of Suffering

Returning to the Scriptures as a helpful guide, we are often remiss as caregivers in forgetting the dynamic of lamentation, which we find throughout God's word. We are so quick to provide comfort or answers that we forget the stage of anger with its accompanying power to release. We do not know how to handle easily the believer's anger toward God, and so we try to "love it away." The lament is an honest acknowledgment of our horror. "O Lord, how long shall I cry for help, and you will not listen? Or cry to you 'Violence' and you will not save?" (Hab. 1:1-2). Jesus himself calls out, "My God, my God, why have you forsaken me?" (Mark 15:34) in a cry of anguish. The lament is our complaint when faced with evil.[7] It is a basic human cry, showing Christ's humanity in the midst of his divinity. In a curious way, it is God calling to God, revealing to us a God who understands suffering. It is also a prayer, an attempt by Jesus to connect somehow with God, to reestablish a relationship that feels tentative amid the pain. It is a way of saying, "Where are you? I need you."

At this point, the person may not believe that he or she has a living relationship with God. As caregivers and pastors we need to give permission for the grieving person to lament. Without this period of legitimate anger toward God, we cannot expect a hurting person to move into the profound questions that will arise before wholeness of spiritual life can be restored. Reminding the bereaved one that God is still present and hears our cry is probably all we can do.

Does suffering, then, happen at random without meaning? No, Rabbi Kushner says, but again the meaning comes from our response. Regularly in everyday life we see occasions of tragedy turned into occasions of love. Mothers Against Drunk Driving (MADD) is an organization founded by women who lost sons and daughters but out of the depth of their grief stood up for children still living and said, "This must stop!" The church that begins a suicide-prevention hotline in its community after a pastor's suicide is another example of tragedy turned into love. The forces of despair and disbelief win out when our response as believers shakes other people's faith in God and the world. We certainly can show our anger, but we should not let our rage become destructive.

The German theologian Dorothee Soelle raises the question, "Does our suffering serve God or the devil?"[8] Does it ultimately lead to forgiveness or does it lead to vengeance? The public response of Jewish mourners reciting the Kaddish, a praising of God for all God's gifts, reminds us that life is good and worth living. When people who were never very strong become so, when such self-serving men as Oskar Schindler, a German who saved hundreds of Jewish factory workers' lives, become heroic, these events point to the true power of God. The community of faith attributes these radical turnarounds to God's transformational power in human existence. From where could this goodness arise otherwise? Sometimes we cannot see God as a healing presence until we look back on the journey. The believer's response of sympathy and righteous indignation in the face of senseless loss is an example of God's compassion and anger working through us. Kushner believes that the reaction of our hearts to such wrong may be the greatest proof of the reality of God.[9] Pastor and author Warren Wiersbe writes: "Quite frankly, there are no explanations for some of the things which happen in life; nor are we required to devise any. People need God more than they need explanation."[10]

Wiersbe agrees with Kushner that the central challenge for us lies not in explaining suffering but rather in facing it and making it a witness *for* God rather than *against* God.[11] He differs from Kushner in believing that God is all-powerful but that God allows suffering as part of human existence and free will. When we embrace an image of God as all-powerful, we turn to God in times of trouble. What can God, in the face of such reality, do for us?

Wiersbe presents a case for four gifts that come from God. First, we are given courage in our faith to face life honestly. We do not have to run away from the horror or become bitter in its wake. Instead we accept the tension that the downside of happiness is sorrow and the joy of life its burdens. That is the way life is. Secondly, God gives us wisdom, in time, to understand what needs to be done. This direction comes through prayer and an openness to God's healing spirit. A third gift is the strength to do what must be done. Almost all of us who have lived through trauma look back in amazement at what God allowed us to do in the moment. Finally, God gives us faith to be patient. God can work even through the brokenness to bring good into the world.[12] By turning the evil to God's good end, God can give meaning to our pain. We can most clearly point to this meaning by the example of God's willingness to suffer on the cross for the good outcome of the redemption of creation. If God could so suffer for us, God can certainly take our tragedies and both feel our hurt and take away the power of evil to hurt us more.

In the wake of trauma in a religious community, the media are thirsting for human-interest stories. Our stories of tragedy, when related in sensitive and caring ways, can potentially offer a great witness to the secular community that reads or hears them. We can only guess how God might use our brokenness for the healing of others. Paul hears God's voice in 2 Cor. 12:9-10: "My grace is sufficient for you, for power is made perfect in weakness. So, I will boast all the more gladly of my weaknesses, so that the power of Christ may dwell in me. Therefore I am content with weaknesses, insults, hardships, persecutions, and calamities for the sake of Christ; for whenever I am weak, then I am strong."

Wiersbe goes on to point out that God didn't take the thorn from Paul's side. Nor did God quickly spare that well-known example of endurance, Job. God can use suffering to mature us. The goal of maturing us is not the cause of our suffering but a by-product. Says Wiersbe: "Puppets and robots don't suffer. People made in God's image do suffer. We are free to submit or free to rebel. How we respond will determine whether suffering will tear us down or build us up."[13] Job's friends went astray in trying to explain instead of encouraging and sympathizing. We cannot build our life on simple formulas. The roles of pastors and caregivers during times of tragedy bring together all elements of the Gospel: forgiveness, divine victory, and atonement. Pastors respond to the challenge of suffering by talking about God and by imitating God's presence through gentle, loving care, thus turning tragedy into love, witnessing for God.

God, Love, and Evil: An Ongoing Tension

Most people's belief systems reflect the tension of trying to balance the existence of suffering and evil with the reality of a loving God. If God really loves us, how can these terrible things happen to us? We cannot resolve this tension neatly, for it remains a mystery. We make judgments from insufficient and ambiguous evidence. The average person in the pew (or average preacher in the pulpit) would likely find any theological explanation totally unsatisfying in response to the question "Why?" Many early theologians influenced by Greek philosophy held that evil was the absence of good, a kind of nonexistence. If God is the ultimate reality and absolute perfection, absolute "good," then the opposite must be absolute imperfection, absolute nonexistence, absolute "evil." It would bring little comfort to the congregation faithfully serving God to be told that the murder of its pastor resulted from "the absence of good." Would members be led to think that God had abandoned this faithful servant during his worst trial? Many readers will find that position in its purest form an offense to the religious awareness of most thoughtful Christians.

Another possibility is that God's power is limited by the divine character of righteousness, truth, and love. God created us as people with free will, but that does not mean that God's exercise of will is as whimsical as ours. When a tornado destroys a church, killing the young daughter of a United Methodist pastor, can we say that the event is "evil" coming from God and the free will of the pastor who brought her child to church? Of course not! Events in the world of nature are not "evil" because *that* world is not under human control. Natural disasters are not planned, nor do they intend harm. It is the world of human will, human choice, and human frailty that best helps us to understand evil as one of the results of a loving Creator's gift of freedom to humankind. God took a risk in making human beings and giving us free will. Not only are we free to refuse God's love, but we are also free to harm God's creation. It is only when the moral order of the world is overthrown and we seek to do harm that "evil" rears its ugly head. It is that subversion which assaults the beauty and order of God's creation.

It is important to explore the use of the term "evil" in our theological discussion of trauma. Evil is approached differently in various faith traditions. For some, evil is a personified "being" often referred to as Satan or the devil. For others, evil is a force that exists within God's universe and comes ultimately under God's authority, but which God allows to manifest for reasons we cannot explain. A third view of evil is that it occurs as a result of human sin. However people understand the source of evil, most of them easily acknowledge that the behavior of human beings can result in evil outcomes. Since so much trauma results from human action, the understanding that evil is manifest in human behavior is expressed frequently in referring to those who cause the suffering of others. Hitler was labeled "the devil incarnate." Mass murderers or child molesters sometimes plead that evil forces or satanic voices made them act violently. We are quick to use the labels of evil when we cannot comprehend another's action.

In *The Death of Satan* psychologist and theologian Andrew Delbanco wonders if Americans still believe in evil in any form. Tracing the church's thinking since medieval times about the personified evil known as "Satan," he concludes that if we did not have such an image, we would probably create one. We want someone outside ourselves to blame for the evil in the world. This idea of a devil also allows us to acknowledge that evil threatens us in personal ways.[14] On the other hand, when we see evil only as a persona or force outside ourselves, we can more easily abdicate responsibility for our actions. Evil, it seems, is the "blamable other" that can always be counted on to spare us the responsibility of examining ourselves.[15]

Unfortunately, blaming some outside source for evil is too easy. Much of human suffering, including situations we label "evil," is the result of factors of our own making. We prefer not to think about our own involvement in systems, in economics, in education. We would rather not know how we contribute to evil by simply turning our heads the other way. Individuals marginalized by society, however, who are subject to violence on a daily basis, who grow up in homes where there is no love, no food, and no hope, are much more likely to act out their anger on the society that did not care.

To acknowledge the role of society is not to say that the one who has committed heinous crimes bears no responsibility for his or her actions. It does point out that evil often mirrors our own insufficient love. We must take responsibility for our own role in evil by grieving with those who have experienced it, and by committing ourselves to addressing the deeper issues that helped unleash it.[16] It is essential to demand the very best in ourselves as we seek to eliminate or overcome such wrong.[17] Breaking the tight grip of evil in our contemporary world means responding to the call to become more deeply involved in the good.

God's ultimate response to evil is victory. "In the world you face persecution. But take courage; I have conquered the world!" (John 16:33). It is easy to read these words when we are not in the throes of trauma. It is much harder when we are crawling blindfolded through the valley of the shadow of death. Moreover, those of us who attempt to live in accordance with God's will find it doubly hard to accept or understand why we should be the victims of such pain. Since human understanding tends to fail us when we are faced with the suffering of those who have done no wrong, we must rely on the grace of God for the faith we cannot find.[18]

Theologian and seminary professor Burton Cooper, writing about the tragic loss of his two children, states, "Grace is loving a loving God when our experience will not let us understand God as loving."[19] The greatest example of this grace is, of course, the sacrifice of Christ. Jesus suffered death at the hands of those whom we call evil. In his death, Jesus presents the failure of his suffering love to compel a loving response. But he overcomes this failure when he identifies with the suffering of the weak as he submits to death on the cross. Out of this scenario, God is able to form a new people shaped by Christ's failure and by his sacrifice. The formation of this "new community," the church, comes from standing against the actions of evil and providing loving support to those who suffer at the hands of evil in its many forms.[20]

The redemptive power of suffering love that we know through the cross calls even the most broken among us to have faith. This point is an important one for Christians to understand. To see the cross as God's victory over evil is to open new perspectives on the nature of evil itself. Evil has such power that nothing other than the death of God's own Son could defeat it. We should be awed by the Cross! The church, therefore, cannot expect to avoid the pain and hurt that God was willing to endure. The church will face evil and suffering. John 15:18 tells us that "the world will hate you." We cannot be free from what God also was willing to endure. The good news is that the church can embody the vulnerable, transforming, healing power of Christ in the world.

This community is essential to our dealing with grief. When churches grieve together, they assure one another that God has not abandoned them in their grief. When my husband lost an older sister in an automobile accident during his final year of seminary, his faith was too shaken to sustain him. I have heard him say often that the church where he was serving as a student intern assured him, "Jay, our faith is strong enough to hold you up—let us do it while you can't." This response reframes the question. It is not about God's power or goodness, but about God's faithfulness. God is a listener who suffers our pain and will not abandon us, and there is *always* one person who can articulate this truth for us, even when we are at different stages of believing it. The primary task of the pastor and other caregivers is to keep open this communication between the grieving church and God.[21]

What About Forgiveness?

Considering this task brings us from thinking about the omnipotence of God and the nature of suffering and evil to the gift of grace and the church as an agent of healing. What, then, can a faithful response be other than forgiveness?

One of the great theologians of the twentieth century, Paul Tillich, understood the power of forgiveness in redeeming great wrong:

> Only a blessing and curse can heal; it is the blessing which changes what seems to be unchangeable—the past. It cannot change the facts; what happened has happened and remains so in all eternity! But the meaning of the facts can be changed by the eternal, and the name of this change is the experience of "forgiveness." If the meaning of the past is changed by forgiveness, its influence on the future

is also changed. The character of curse is taken away from it. It has become a blessing by the transforming power of forgiveness.[22]

Forgiveness is a true theological term. Books written on trauma from a solely psychological perspective rarely mention "forgiveness"; when they do, it is equated with "acceptance." It is within the body of Christ, the church, where we raise the hard questions about forgiveness. When hearts are broken and anger runs rampant, it is difficult to preach or hear the call to forgiveness. I would caution the reader that each situation is unique and the timing for such discussion is critical. Addressed too soon, it falls at best on inattentive ears. The wrongly timed suggestion of forgiving the perpetrator will more likely fuel the fires of hostility. Recognizing that anger can be a preparation for healing, we cannot deny that the foundation of God's continual love for us rests in part on God's forgiving nature. At the right time, God's time, we must at least begin the process of forgiving. For some, ultimate reconciliation may not be possible in this lifetime.

God's forgiveness of us is truly amazing. God's relentless search for us, calling us to repentance, but still loving us when our hearts are too hardened to change—these are all signs of the nature of a loving creator. God's love for us is totally unconditional. But we humans are not God. We do not seek out, nor do we easily forgive—especially when our world has collapsed at the hands of one perceived as "evil." Forgiveness takes time. After we demand that God punish our enemies, we pray, "God help my unforgiving heart." How grateful we should be that God's forgiveness of us is greater than our ability to repent or forgive others.

When in John 23:34 we hear Jesus cry from the cross, "Father, forgive them; for they do not know what they are doing," we frail humans cringe. Encountering the perpetrators of trauma in our own lives, we believe that they knew *exactly* what they were doing. We harbor anger and vengeance as if they were precious tools for survival. We seek retribution, punishment, sometimes even the death of those who have caused us pain. It is only God's love and patience that can slowly lead us to an awareness that forgiveness is our calling and that our healing and our ability to forgive are intrinsically linked in God's provision for our care.

In the devotional journal *Weavings*, Marjorie Thompson suggests that Christians often confuse forgiveness with "forgetting." Forgiveness does not mean denying our hurt. We must acknowledge that the impact of someone's actions has been destructive to our life. We cannot "just forget about it." Forgiveness is a choice that we may, in time, be able to make, but not without cost. "Forgiveness," Thompson says, "is a decision to call forth and rebuild that love which is the only authentic ground of any human relationship...Indeed, it is only because God continually calls forth and rebuilds this love with us that we are capable of doing so with one another. To forgive is to participate in the mystery of God's love."[23] When we forgive, we are not trying to push aside the memory of what has happened. We are, instead, preventing the past from cursing us to a life of bitterness and misery. Retaliation rarely brings joy.[24] In the end, the alternatives to forgiveness are just too destructive. When our forgiveness is grounded in God's forgiveness of us, it has tremendous power to rebuild and renew our shattered lives.

When Mrs. Young Shik Jung was murdered in the back room of the small grocery store she and her husband owned in Indianapolis, public attention was focused on the tensions between the African-American and Korean-American communities. Mrs. Jung had been an active member of the Indianapolis Korean Presbyterian Church and president of its women's association. Her husband was an elder. When an arrest was made, an interview with Mrs. Jung's son was shown repeatedly on local television stations. The son, a student at Purdue University and an active Christian, was asked what his mother might say, knowing that an arrest had been made. He quickly responded, "She's smiling, because, you see, she has already forgiven him."

At the close of *When Bad Things Happen to Good People*, Harold Kushner raises the questions: "Are you capable of forgiving and accepting a world which has disappointed you? Can you love God again and God's world and see it as capable of goodness and beauty?" The ability to forgive and the ability to love again are the weapons God has given us to fight the evil that surrounds us and to live fully and bravely in a broken world.[25] Forgiveness is the first step toward reconciliation; through God's grace we can be reconciled with God. Then we can reconcile our vision of life as good. Forgiveness is what we work toward in the healing process.

I would stress again the importance of possessing, *before* trauma strikes, a theological framework that can address the tension between belief in a loving God and the presence of evil; a theology of suffering;

and an understanding of grace and forgiveness. Pastors in particular need not shy from these topics, fearing they may be "downers" to most people. Indeed, it is the church's job to prepare its members with strong foundations for the rocking of their faith during times of trauma. But when tragedy does strike, the sensitive minister or caregiver offers a hand to hold and a faith to lean on as the blows of life threaten to over-come even the most staunch believers. Our God is a God of compassion, suffering, love, forgiveness, and hope. What more could we ask?

CHAPTER 2

The Psychology of Trauma

Hearts pound, mouths dry like spit on stone, ears ring in deafening alarm: Anxiety is tethering us to the violence done to us. Victims once, Lord, we fear being victims forever unless we get a grip, get control, get over it.

> —Margaret Anne Huffman,
> *"Through the Valley…" Prayers for Violent Times*, p. 109

Picture a summer afternoon at the lake. People paddle canoes through the peaceful water, enjoying the ride. Some canoes are in good repair. The baggage they carry is neatly packed. Coolers and picnic baskets are carefully secured to keep them from tumbling around during the trip. Other canoes look to be poorly maintained. Belongings roll loose; the canoes appear unbalanced. Suddenly a meteor drops from the sky. The canoes that take a direct hit are destroyed or damaged, no matter how well kept and secured. Some canoes, those well packed and in good repair and far enough from the meteor's point of impact, make it through the crash. What happens to the others, especially those without the durability or maintenance to survive the tidal wave?

This analogy was used by Kim Walton, coordinator of the Adolescent Clinic of Wishard Hospital in Indianapolis, to describe the impact of trauma on a group. Everyone will be affected. The more direct the hit, the more likely damage will result. The healthier the individual or system, the better chance the person or congregation has to survive the aftermath. We know that the waves of crisis are far-reaching. Even bystanders on the shore can be affected.

In a 1992 article for *Employee Assistance Program Digest*, C. A. Frolkey, a specialist in personnel issues, defines the difference between a critical incident or periodic crisis and a true traumatic occurrence. Both critical incidents and traumas are emotionally charged. The difference is that a crisis is *expected* in the course of one's daily life. Regular crisis often involves loss to others. Trauma is the result of an unanticipated and sudden event and always involves significant *personal* loss, which leaves the individual feeling devastated and out of control. Critical incidents and traumatic events can overlap. Consider, for example, the emergency worker who discovers at the scene of an accident that the victim is her brother.[1]

From Homer's *Odyssey* to Samuel Pepys's diary entries describing the disastrous London fire of 1666, the profound effects of extreme stress on human beings have been documented. Although Sigmund Freud noted the long-term effects of childhood psychological trauma as early as the nineteenth century, it has been only in the aftermath of the great wars of this century that concerted scientific effort has been made to understand the symptoms resulting from extreme stress.[2]

This chapter will explore trauma that goes beyond the crisis events of everyday life, no matter how difficult those might seem at the time. For our purposes, trauma is the large-scale effect of a sudden, unexpected crisis event on a large group of people—namely, the system we call a *congregation*. Trauma is initially overwhelming. It permanently changes the environment and the lives of all who exist within it.

Since congregations are groups formed by individuals, it is important to understand the difference between individual trauma and group trauma. Both can put into motion powerful emotional forces. These include a sense of smallness and feelings of extreme vulnerability or terror. Fear and panic can aggravate the emotional dynamics of pain and loss. Unlike personal trauma, which must initially be addressed as an individual, mass trauma can benefit from the healing presence of other group members. The healing of the individual affected by a group trauma can be hastened if the individual remains connected to the courage and healing journey of the larger group.[3] The strong group affiliation of the Jewish people is often attributed to their ability to survive traumas such as the Holocaust together. The recognition of shared pain provides a framework for healing. So does the opportunity to draw on the courage and support of those gathered to support the survivors. For these reasons, congregational gatherings, to be discussed at length later, are essential following a traumatic incident.

In reality, disasters have more effect on some individuals than on others. People differ in their capacity to respond to the demands of trauma. Individual reactions can range from mild to severe and, when highly dysfunctional, may persist. Reactions have been documented up to five years following a nuclear accident and 14 years after a town was destroyed by a dam collapse.[4] One study of people evacuated after a cyclone in Darwin, Australia, showed that a week after their removal 58 percent could be classified as psychiatric cases. Twelve weeks later the number of cases diagnosed stood at 41 percent. A similar study found 70 percent of disaster victims in Sri Lanka deeply disturbed. A month later 46 percent remained in that category. It seems that a significant number of people have not improved even three months after a trauma.[5] These personal responses can include a sense of shame, isolation ("Everyone is over this except me"), self-blame, and the belief that no one truly understands the depth of loss. If these statistics are transferable to congregations, they suggest that almost half the members of a church will continue to suffer severe traumatic stress symptoms for months following a traumatic event.

Is the world benevolent or malevolent? Is the world meaningful or meaningless? Am I worthy or unworthy? Are other people trustworthy or untrustworthy? These four questions are the most prevalent in the emotional struggle of those who are traumatized.[6]

The Stress Response

The American psychological community began to apply the label "posttraumatic stress disorder" (PTSD) shortly after World War II, but it did not become common until public attention was focused on the returning Vietnam War veterans and the extreme difficulty many faced returning to postservice existence. Situations that can result in PTSD include criminal victimization, natural disasters, disasters wrought by human action such as war or terrorism, catastrophic accidents, and vocations that place individuals in life-or-death situations. The best single predictor of PTSD is the severity of the traumatic experience.[7] We know also that the effect is more pronounced when the trauma is inflicted intentionally than when it is accidental.[8] The American Psychiatric Association's *Diagnostic and Statistical Manual of Mental Disorders* cites five criteria for a PTSD diagnosis:

1. The person must have witnessed or experienced a serious threat to life or physical well-being.

2. The person must reexperience the event in some way. Such phenomena include recurrent or intrusive recollections of the event; recurrent dreams; flashbacks; and intense reactions or distress to smells, sounds, or visual images that symbolize or resemble an aspect of the event.

3. The person must persistently avoid stimuli associated with the trauma or experience a numbing of general responsiveness.

4. The person must experience difficulty falling or staying asleep, irritability or outbursts of anger, difficulty concentrating, hypervigilance, or exaggerated or startled responses—all referred to as "increased arousal."

5. Symptoms must have lasted at least a month.

Some of these symptoms may be present in individuals who are not technically diagnosed as post-traumatic stress disorder victims.

I experienced several of these symptoms myself after murders in the presbytery where I serve as executive—an event related in greater detail in chapter three. A pastor and his wife were killed in their home, which was then set on fire. After the trauma had subsided, I realized that I had been taking a different route home from my office, one that kept me from driving past the church the late pastor had served. Further reflection disclosed that ten months after the murders I had still not returned to the scene of the violence, although I knew the fire damage had been repaired and the house was now on the market. After attending World Communion Sunday morning worship at the church, almost a year after the tragedy, I walked back through the empty sanctuary on my way to the spot where my car was parked. Suddenly I was overwhelmed by the presence of the murdered pastor, and I almost saw him standing in the pulpit preaching.

I thought the tears had been long since washed away, but I was mistaken. The memory of many Christmas Eves rushed back as I opened the door to leave, and the pastor's "memory" shook hands with me one more time as I left. Was I exhibiting signs of PTSD? Perhaps I suffered from what is called "partial PTSD." My encounter with the past was very real in those moments. It indicated to me that my own grief and healing were not yet complete.

Our goals in responding to trauma should include:

1. Restoring equilibrium to the setting.

2. Reconnecting individuals to their coping skills.

3. Promoting the most positive outcome possible for all involved.

4. When possible, preventing long-term maladaptive stress reactions that can result from failure to address trauma at the outset.

In most situations this response should occur through relationships that are both formal (therapeutic) and informal (with nonprofessional caregivers).

Crisis intervention, which pastors might provide, is *not* therapy. Most pastors are ill-prepared to provide the care and guide the recovery process that needs to occur after trauma. Therapy, which will likely be needed later, is inappropriate initially because people in trauma are highly stressed. They are often out of touch with their own thoughts, feelings, and coping skills. Severely traumatized people do not feel safe, and therapy cannot be effective until individuals feel safe enough to explore the psychological effects of the event. The rare exception to this general principle should be made when a person is affected so severely that he or she cannot function. Then professional care should be sought as soon as possible. Seventeen symptoms have been identified; immediate intervention by a professional is needed when several of these are present:

1. Disorientation as to date, day of the week, events of the past 24 hours.

2. Excessive concern over little things, preoccupation with one idea.

3. Denial of the severity of the situation, resulting in a belief that the event never occurred.

4. Visual or auditory flashbacks that are confused with reality.

5. Self-doubt expressed verbally in such words as "going crazy" or "losing my mind."

6. Difficulty carrying out basic life functions such as eating, sleeping, or dressing.

7. Mild confusion that has escalated to bizarre, irrational beliefs on which the person acts.

8. Crying that becomes uncontrollable hysteria.

9. Anger or self-blame that becomes fear or threats to harm oneself or others.

10. Numbing that results in complete withdrawal with little or no emotional response.

11. Appropriate expression of despair that deepens to include thoughts of self-destruction.

12. Restlessness or excitement that becomes unfocused agitation.

13. Excessive talking or uncontrollable nervous laughter.

14. Frequent retelling of the incident that has become constant or ritualistic.

15. Pacing, hand-wringing, or fist-clenching that is ritualistic or uncontrolled.

16. Continual disheveled appearance over time, reflecting an inability to care for oneself.

17. Irritability that becomes destructive.[9]

As caregivers in the traumatic situation who may not be mental-health professionals, we should remember that traumatized people need to talk about what happened. They need to relate the situation to other events in their lives. They often need to explain the incident to themselves so that they can acknowledge it. Acceptance cannot precede acknowledgment. Initially, telling the story over and over has a therapeutic effect. This retelling should subside, however, within a reasonable amount of time. Individuals should be encouraged to continue their usual routine as much as possible while recovering. Although there will be a period when everything stops, it is important to help individuals—and the congregation as a whole—to return to normal patterns as soon as possible. A normal routine provides comfort, support, and stability at a highly unstable time. In all congregational settings discussed in this book, worship continued as usual on the Sunday morning after the incident. Community programs, such as nursery schools, were back on regular schedules within a few days of the trauma.

A dynamic called "delayed stress" sometimes strikes those whose stress reactions do not appear at the time of the trauma. It is not unusual for people to hold up fairly well during the immediate aftermath, only to fall apart later. Often these are people who have a role to play in the days immediately following the event. Clergy, secretaries, and custodial staff all have to continue functioning to plan prayer services, the memorial service, and community gatherings. Bulletins have to be typed, phone lines answered, and chairs set up. In one case study, a person was heard to say, "I don't have time to grieve right now—there's too much to do." Such people put their emotions on hold until the crisis is under control. They experience a delayed response by choice. But some stress is delayed not by choice but by the individual's failed coping mechanisms.

Delayed stress can occur weeks, months, or even years after the trauma. The symptoms are like those of acute stress but are not incident-specific. Delayed stress can be difficult to recognize if considerable time has passed since the trauma. One key to identifying delayed stress is to consult the symptom list for PTSD, when such symptoms persist beyond a year to 18 months. If the trauma victim's current behavior has changed substantially from behavior before the incident, chances are that he or she is suffering from delayed stress and should be referred to a mental health professional.[10]

When the Trauma Is Homicide

When the trauma involves homicide, additional needs arise for the survivors (family, coworkers, and close friends) and to a lesser degree for the congregation. There is no way to prepare for what people will go through—no way to comprehend that death can come so violently, swiftly at the brutal hands of another human being. The survivors of a murder victim have special needs that include:

1. Empowerment to gain control of one's life.

2. Access to a supportive environment in which people are free to express their emotions.

3. Knowledge of the loss on the part of supportive others.

4. Knowledge and understanding of the design and purpose of law-enforcement agencies and the criminal justice system.

5. Integration of the murder into one's mental framework.

6. Opportunity to work through grief, becoming as emotionally stable as possible.[11]

Most people dealing with loss begin with the sixth item, the grieving process. When homicide is involved, individuals must meet other needs before the sixth can occur. Most survivors grieving the loss of a homicide victim should be referred to professionals immediately. Early assistance can be effective. Group therapy is also helpful, once the person has stabilized. The mutual support of others in the congregation is helpful and might suffice for people who were not close to the victim, but such support will not by itself effectively address the deep wounds of close friends, associates, and family members of the victim.

The other emotion prevalent in homicide or other violent traumas is fear. The world is no longer a safe place. The staff and many members of the congregation mentioned earlier were frightened by the murders of their pastor and his wife. Countless church members mentioned that they purchased security systems the next week. Even with increased security at the church, some members did not want to attend evening meetings. Parents of preschoolers wondered whether they should send their children to the day school.

Fear was not limited to primary survivors, those closely associated with the congregation. It permeated our presbytery. The week after the event I had pastors calling to ask if they were safe. Rumors were rampant—that the pastor and his wife were killed because of their position on controversial denominational issues, or that the murders were part of a serial attack against Presbyterian clergy sparked by the denomination's position on social concerns.

The secondary "survivors" included the children of ministers in our area. One six-year-old daughter of a pastor refused to go into the house when the family returned home to find the garage door standing open. When the mother asked her why, the child replied, "The television said those people who hurt that minister may have been in the garage." Fear brings on feelings of vulnerability, which affect everything in the environment for some time to come. Caregivers need to be aware of this state, acknowledging the feeling without escalating the panic. Fear, although it may be legitimate, is not always rational.

When the Trauma Is Suicide

When the trauma involves suicide, identifying those affected is more difficult. They often include people who are not part of the church—teachers, counselors, sports teams, and social groups of the deceased. These people are often difficult to find because they don't talk about the death easily. They are deeply wounded by the suddenness of their loved one's or friend's act. They have not had time to prepare for the loss, even when they had been aware of depression or despondency. They may feel a sense of shame in the family or within the larger community, fearing that others will hold them responsible for not saving the deceased. This feeling of shame or responsibility is compounded by fears that they should have been able to prevent the act. They often go over the past days or weeks before the death searching for missed signs or signals. Suicide often brings out family secrets or confronts myths of "the perfect family," "a model Christian home," or, when the person who has committed suicide is a religious professional, "God's chosen one."

Issues common to mourners of a suicide include a perpetual need to search for clues to reasons for the suicide, profound guilt, altered social relationships related to a perceived stigma, complex and often incomplete grief patterns, the unconscious idea that suicide is a way of solving problems, and erosion of the capacity to trust others.[12] The most effective way to assist the grieving ones is to encourage them to join a professionally led support group for those who have lost someone through suicide and to engage in individual therapy. Since the congregation as a whole can exhibit these symptoms, it is important that opportunities to address the issues through classes and small-group ministries be provided. Mental-health professionals can be asked to assist the congregation with these programs and services.

The Many Dimensions of Grief

Loss results in grief. In their book on grief and loss, Anderson and Mitchell write: "To be a follower of Christ is to love life and to value people and things that God has given to us in such a way that losing them brings sadness. Friends move away; children die; buildings are torn down; dreams go unfulfilled; communities change. Even when we know that endings are coming, they come as unwelcome surprises."[13] When the loss results from a traumatic incident, grief is even more profound. Grief is a state of being. It is not an event but a normal response to a loss beyond our control. The "long ghastly day" seems to go on forever. Because of the depth of the wound, even one's sense of self often seems unfamiliar.[14] Grief affects the whole person—physically, emotionally, cognitively, spiritually, and behaviorally.

The symptoms of grief are well known to most readers. Initially the shock and numbness are almost welcome. We know that the mind can accept only so much troubling new information. The shock that immediately follows a trauma will often help us to hear the news and yet still function. Shock quickly wears off, and the emotions take over. We cry and cry—and cry some more. Tears are an important part of grieving and should not be discouraged. In fact, the Bible often mentions weeping as one of God's healing gifts. Psalm 56:8 says, "You have kept count of my tossings; put my tears in your bottle. Are they not in your record?" Tears tend to embarrass us when shed in public places, or when we think we should no longer cry. The grief that follows trauma may yield tears for many days, weeks, even years; and that is OK. It is important for caregivers and others who can influence the grieving environment to give permission for crying.

Anger is another common emotion in grieving. When anger can be directed toward a perpetrator or an incident, the anger seems logical to people. In situations where anger is directed toward the one who committed suicide or toward the homicide victim, it becomes more complex. Anger at the one who "has left" is a natural reaction. A parishioner who had been close to her murdered pastor was disturbed at the anger she felt toward him for "leaving her" until she realized that this reaction was connected with the loss of her father. As caregivers we need to remember that anger embarrasses those who feel it. They are ashamed to be "mad" at the one who is dead or has suffered. Yet the feeling is real and should be acknowledged without judgment to help the grieving one move beyond it.

Most of us also understand that guilt often accompanies loss. Whether the trauma involves the death of one or many, we may feel guilty for all the things we "should" have done or said. Sometimes we feel guilt because we naïvely (or rightly) believe we could have prevented the event. Asking "Why didn't I?" or telling oneself "I should have" is rarely helpful. A certain amount of guilt feeling is normal, but a person unable to accept the past may need additional assistance in this part of the grief journey.

The need for assistance also applies when the grieving person becomes severely depressed. Depression may result from suppressed grief. One needs to ask if depression seems normal under the circumstances. If the depression is constant and prolonged, outside help may be needed.[15] Laughter may seem an unusual emotion to consider in a section on grief, but it is an important reaction to discuss. With no release, the mind and body reach their limits of endurance. The "wake" that precedes or follows a funeral in many ethnic communities offers the opportunity to remember, to tell stories, and to laugh. When the loss has been the result of trauma, laughter may seem inappropriate. However, laughter releases endorphins in our body—naturally occurring chemicals that promote a feeling of well-being and hasten the healing process.[16] In the memorial to one murdered pastor, several people told stories that illustrated his robust sense of humor and brought a chuckle to those gathered. One newspaper report termed the service more of a "celebration of life" than the morbid gathering anticipated. Isn't that what the Christian Church believes—that no matter how terrible the tragedy, God promises us life eternal?

Factors Affecting Grief

The outcome of grief will be affected by:

1. Developmental and age-related factors. (Example: The death of a child affects a parent differently than the death of the adult's own parent.)

2. The circumstances surrounding death or loss. (Example: A homicide or suicide is more difficult to reconcile than a natural death.)

3. Physical health status of the bereaved. (Example: Coping with personal illness may affect the grief process.)

4. Mental, emotional, and developmental status of the bereaved. (Example: A person suffering from depression will likely struggle more with grief issues.)

5. Certain social, cultural, or ethnic factors (Example: A fire in a "sacred" place or a racially motivated arson provokes a response different from that prompted by an electrical fire in a home.)

6. Historical factors. (Example: If previous pastors have been guilty of sexual misconduct, a current allegation will spark stronger emotions.)

7. Concurrent losses. (Example: When a beloved pastor retires after 30 years and the church building is leveled by a tornado two months later, people will probably grieve more deeply.)

8. Person's belief system. (Example: A person who has perhaps wished the deceased gone feels guilty that the wish came true and grieves differently.)

9. The nature of the relationship with the loss or person (Example: The closer the relationship to the deceased or to those affected by the tragedy, the greater the grief response.)

10. Education, occupational, and economic status of the bereaved (Example: A mental health worker may have more tools available than most people to move through the stages of grief quickly.)

11. Degree to which others depend on or need the grieving person. (Example: The grieving pastor who has to plan a memorial service will probably set aside grief temporarily.)

12. The ability of the person to express grief. (Example: A person unaccustomed to showing emotion will grieve differently from those who express emotion easily.)[17]

Although it is important to address grief corporately in a congregational setting, it is also crucial to remember that individuals are in many different stages of grief. The following incident illustrates how people grieve differently and move through grief at different tempos.

After a pastor's violent death, the local judicatory recommended to the congregation's governing board that a "transitional" head of staff be called to serve the congregation for at least three years. This person would serve as interim pastor, but the search for an installed pastor would not begin for at least two years—a year for healing and stabilizing the congregation followed by a thorough study of its mission. Some members reacted strongly to the group's decision to follow the advice. Some key congregational leaders who were not involved in the action believed such a strategy to be tantamount to treading water and declared that the church needed to "get on with it."

When, as a judicatory official, I learned that these vocal opponents were mostly participants in a weekly men's prayer breakfast, I asked for an invitation to address the group. As I presented the rationale for the longer interim period, I looked around the room and noticed that most of those present were of the generation that fought World War II. I asked those who had served in that war to raise their hands. Almost every man did. I pointed out that in combat when a buddy was injured or killed, they had to keep going—the stakes were so high that they couldn't afford to stop and grieve. I suggested that this pattern of bucking up and moving ahead was a learned one that had served them well in battle. Heads nodded in agreement. Then I pointed out that many members of the congregation had not served in any war and had no other experience to parallel theirs. For these individuals, grief had a different dynamic. They couldn't go on until the emotional issues were addressed. I told the story of a woman who, eight weeks after the violent death, was still frightened to get up during the night and would awaken her husband before leaving the bedroom.

The grief pattern of these faithful servants of Christ was being affected by some of the factors listed above. They had learned a generational response in a specific historical era, and it continued to determine their expression of grief and reaction to loss. With this understanding of the transitional period strategy, the prayer-breakfast participants became effective spokespeople for the board's decision.

Congregational Grief

It is important to point out that trauma and grief are suffered both by the individuals who make up the congregation and by the church as a whole. Because grief is unique to each person, the point where an entire congregation finds itself in the process is not easily assessed. It is easy to confuse where the congregation may be with where a few highly visible or articulate individuals seem to be. At the same time, we know from the work of Edwin Friedman in his book *Generation to Generation* that individuals are often drawn to a church because the "system" of that congregation reflects their own "family system." We face loss of any kind as we learned to face it in our family settings. We first learn about grief from those with whom we've shared life. Some families mourn openly and freely. Others keep grief inside and choose not to show their pain.

Congregations have patterns and personalities just as families do. It is fascinating that congregations do not vary these patterns significantly over several generations. As caregivers we need to know something about this church "family." Healthy congregations seem energized and able to approach challenges with an inner strength. Less healthy congregations appear "stuck," depressed, or pessimistic.[18] The healthier the congregation when trauma strikes, the better able it will be to manage grief. Other factors to observe include its patterns of managing conflict and of dealing with hardship or crisis. Knowing these patterns will help us not only in the short run of trauma management, but also in the days ahead as we attempt to assess the grieving and healing process.

That the Christian is promised eternity with God does not mean we should not grieve. The difference is that Christians grieve in hope. Paul suggests as much in 1 Thess. 4:13: "You may not grieve as others do who have no hope." Jesus himself grieved the loss of his dear friend Lazarus. Perhaps the Christian is more able to grieve because our promise is anchored in one from whom we will never be separated. God's presence provides a shelter. It is this promise and hope that free us to grieve more rather than less.

The healing process we call "grieving" involves facing the reality of loss and letting go. It involves experiencing the pain of grief—the hurt, the tears, the agony. It means adjusting and eventually accepting an altered environment. The deceased is never returning. The burnt building can be rebuilt, but the memories in the old one cannot be replaced. We know that healing has taken place when the grieving person is finally able to reinvest in the future.[19]

Three Faces of Tragedy

*Help us to heal by retelling our stories and replaying the scenes
until they become no more and no less than a part of the past, like
a scar on a shoulder. Veterans keep memories and mementos in a
scrapbook on a shelf; we put ours there now, too. If we need to
look at it again, turn its pages with us, O God, reminding us how
brave we are, how far we've come since we lived in the battle
zones.*

> –Margaret Anne Huffman,
> *"Through the Valley..." Prayers for Violent Times*, p. 174

It was a rainy night, balmy for December. I had gone to bed early, enjoying the fact that it was close enough to Christmas that demands on my
time as executive of the Presbytery of Whitewater Valley were almost
nonexistent. I was jolted back to consciousness after midnight by a sudden interruption—the ringing telephone that stops the heart of even the
deepest sleeper. Such calls rarely bring good news. This one was no exception. I recognized the voice on the phone as that of Jerry Weber, parish associate at Northminster Presbyterian Church in Indianapolis and
spouse of Donna Wells, the associate pastor. My first thought was that
something had happened to one of their young children. Jerry had re-
cently accepted a position involving travel, and Donna had made the
difficult decision to resign from Northminster, effective the end of the
year, to be home with her family. Donna loved Northminster and had a
special relationship with Fred and Cleta Mathias, the senior pastor and
his wife, who had become adopted grandparents for the Wells-Weber

children. It was especially difficult for Donna to leave at this point in
the church's life, because Fred had shared with the pastoral staff his
intention to retire in June.

"Don Durrett just called and said we have a real tragedy on our
hands. I'm going to let you talk to Donna." Through the tears and tone
of panic I was able to make out that there had been a fire and to hear the
crushing announcement, "They're dead!" As the relief of talking to
someone took hold, Donna was able to tell me that Don Durrett, her
associate pastor colleague who had served Northminster for 30 years,
had been contacted by the Marion County Sheriff's Department to verify that the Rev. Dr. C. Frederick Mathias and his wife, Cleta, lived at
7215 Dean Road. The sheriff broke the news: The residence was on
fire, and the two bodies found inside were believed to be that of the
pastor and his wife. Looking at the clock, I saw that it was 1:30 A.M. I
told Donna and Jerry that I would join Don at the Mathias home so that
he would not be there alone. I promised to call them as soon as I had
more information. Hanging up the phone, I turned to my husband, Jay,
and said, "There's something wrong here. Fred and Cleta would have a
smoke detector and couldn't have been asleep long enough not to have
heard it." Jay, the more level-headed one of our family, suggested that I
was upset and jumping to conclusions.

Looking back, one always finds the immediate moments of crisis
fascinating. Surprisingly, I had the foresight to grab clothes from the
closet quickly and to throw my makeup into a bag. I knew I would not
be returning home for a long, long time.

The drive to the Mathias residence was quiet. As we approached
the neighborhood, I said again, "Jay, something's wrong here. There's
been foul play." He lovingly assured me that I had no reason to believe
that. Pulling up to the block, we saw that the street had been closed off
by barricades. Parking along the cross street, we could already see the
lights from the fire trucks, the flashing police vehicles, and—my heart
sank—news vans from all the Indianapolis television stations. As we
walked up the circular driveway, we were met by Don and his wife,
Nancy. After emotional hugs Don told me the deaths were not accidental.
We got into the Durrett car and waited for the chaplain of the sheriff's
department to finish his conversation and come join us. At that time all
we knew was that the fire department had been called by a neighbor at
about 11:10 P.M. Firefighters, discovering the bodies, immediately called

the sheriff's department. Don and Nancy, who were called shortly after midnight, rushed to the site.

The wait in the car was full of pained small talk. What had happened? We rehearsed the events of the previous evening over and over. We knew the Mathiases had attended the annual Advent worship service sponsored jointly by Northminster Presbyterian and the neighboring congregation, Christ the King Roman Catholic Church. What could have happened to cause a fire as early as 11:00 P.M.? I got out of the car and walked around to the front of the house. Crime tape had already been put in place, but I could easily see into the foyer, brightly lit by the investigating officers. It was the same familiar entranceway I had walked through on many social occasions. No one could guess the horror that lay inside. I was flooded with memories.

When the chaplain on duty came to our car, he told us that not only had Fred and Cleta been killed; their murder was also an act of extreme violence. They had been accosted even before removing their coats; apparently they had surprised the perpetrators.

The chaplain had not yet been able to reach the Mathias children, who lived in the Northeast. He requested that we not speak with anyone until the family had been notified. I suggested that we go to the church and begin to plan the difficult task of breaking the news to the congregation. We had called Donna Wells earlier from the car phone to update her and to suggest that she and her husband call a neighbor to come stay with their children. We now called and asked them to meet us at Northminster. Minutes seemed like hours, but it was only 3:00 A.M.

The story unfolded slowly. We went to the church, waited, and prayed. The chaplain joined us. In our presence he called Mark Mathias, Fred and Cleta's oldest son. He had waited until the Delaware State Police had arrived at Mark's home—standard procedure for an out-of-state homicide. The news of the death is shared, but the chaplain to the law-enforcement department where the death occurred is the one who gives the details. I was startled to hear the chaplain say, "Mark, I have some information for you which will be difficult to hear. Last evening sometime between 9:00 and 11:00 your parents were bound and murdered with an ax in their home." This was the first we had heard of the actual details of their death. A wave of disbelief washed over our small gathering. How could this be? Who would have done such an unfathomable act?

It is important to note that in many trauma settings not all the information is immediately available. We learned the unfortunate details in bits and pieces over a period of several days. When an "exposé" article appeared in the *Indianapolis Star* six months later, new pieces of information emerged which we, the intimates in this situation, had not known. One of the biggest challenges, particularly when the tragedy is a crime, is the dissemination and protection of information. We learned that cellular phones are often monitored by the media, as are fire- and police-radio communications. Sometimes information that might be withheld to check the authenticity of tips in the case ends up in the public domain and loses its value. We were cautioned about discussing the case on a cellular phone.

As the horror of what we had just learned sank in, I began to ponder what I had heard. This wasn't just a murder; it was a nightmare. We had agreed earlier to begin contacting the session (the governing board of a Presbyterian congregation) at 4:00 A.M. for a called meeting of the session at 5:30 A.M. I now suggested that we only say, "There has been a terrible tragedy at the church. We need you to come for an emergency meeting at 5:30." We hoped to give everyone the information at the same time. To the credit of each, by the grace of God, not one person asked us what had happened. We also called three other staff members to join us for the meeting.

I then called my two presbytery staff colleagues, told them what had happened, and recruited them to begin calling clergy in the presbytery who could assist in pastoral care. They were assigned in teams of two for one-hour shifts beginning at 8:00 A.M. for the remainder of the day.

While waiting for the elders to arrive, we developed our plan for the session meeting. Don would thank them for coming and then turn the meeting over to me. I would read a short Scripture passage and then inform them of what had happened. Following the example of the sheriff's department chaplain, I would give the facts as we knew them, including details of the murder. I would then suggest the decisions that had to be made immediately. While waiting, we had rolled a television into the church office. We were shocked that the local 5:00 a.m. news led with the story of the murders. We braced ourselves: Some of the elders would already know. The leaders of the church, some accompanied by spouses, began to arrive. It was easy to tell who had already heard. No one, however, asked any questions. We asked those who obviously knew not to tell others, emphasizing that we'd like to convey the information to all at one time. The mood was somber. Someone came in with a newspaper. The headline read, "The Nighmare Before Christmas." A quick read of the article revealed graphic and disturbing details of the murders. I knew it was going to be an awful day.

My husband stayed in the office to handle the phone and to be present if people came into the church while the session was meeting. By the time the meeting began, the custodial staff had arrived and a few Northminster members had come by to offer help.

No conflict intervention, no all-night hospital vigil, no testimony in a civil case against a church was as difficult for me as that session meeting. The faces of those who had already heard said it all. Those who did not know had come to the church assuming that something had happened to Fred—a heart attack, a car accident. No one was prepared for the awful truth.

Don Durrett thanked the elders for coming on short notice and made special note that no one was absent. He then asked everyone to join him in prayer. The petition was one that acknowledged our need of God during times of heartbreak and asked for God's guidance and healing presence in the midst of tragedy. Since I was no stranger to the Northminster Session, little introduction of me was necessary. I read a psalm and then, as gently but straightforwardly as possible, gave the session all the information we had. This included:

1. What time the Mathiases left the service at Christ the King. Donna Wells, who had participated in the service, had visited with them in the parking lot before leaving.

2. What time the phone call about the fire was made to Don Durrett.

3. What was discovered at the scene. We spared them no details. The account in the newspaper about the crime scene itself made this point essential. We wanted to verify accurate information as we understood it.

4. A report on how the adult Mathias children had been informed.

After an opportunity for questions (there were few), we proceeded to the

morning's pressing issues. The associate pastors and I had already agreed
on several things that the session might do. I recommended that:

1. We hold a prayer meeting that evening at 7:00.

2. Leaders organize a telephone tree to call all members of
   Northminster, informing them of the service.

3. We appoint one member of the session as "spokesperson" to deal
   with the media.

The session unanimously approved all the recommendations and
appointed as spokesperson Mark Moore, a young attorney who had re-
cently moved from the Indiana governor's staff to a local firm. Mark
had extensive experience with the media through his work at the state-
house. One of the elders, Bama Kennedy, offered to organize the telephone tree. Since Northminster has 1,700 members, an electronic
"calling system" was often used. The system takes about three days to
call all families. Bama mobilized volunteers, and every family had received a personal call by 3:00 P.M.

When we adjourned the session meeting, the temperature had
dropped, and the rain had turned to snow. I remember thinking that the
morning's whiteness was a sharp contrast to the darkness we were all
feeling.

Immediately after the session meeting the pastoral staff and I met
with Mark Moore to plan strategy and statements to the press and media.
We agreed that the church's position would be one of openness and
vulnerability and that we would also exemplify in our public presence
the healing and forgiving love of Christ—even in the face of such a
despicable act.

The two associate pastors and I then began to plan the evening
prayer service. Although it would not be closed to the public, we agreed
that it would be presented as a service for the members of Northminster
to provide solace and support. A memorial service for the Mathiases
would come later in the week after the family had had time to make
decisions. We agreed that the initial service would be one of prayer and
meditation and that the worship leaders would include only the two associate pastors, the parish associate, the seminary intern, and me.

From the beginning we chose not to involve leadership from outside the congregation, believing that familiar faces would be most comforting to the congregation. (The only exception to this decision came on the first two Sundays after the murders. The associate pastors were not yet emotionally ready to preach, and we chose to invite individuals known to the congregation who had special skills in pastoral care and healing.) My presence, as the presbytery executive, represented the link between the church and the larger supportive community of our Presbyterian family and tradition. I have never been more thankful to be part of a connectional denomination. My frequent visits in my role as pastor to the presbytery provided an established relationship upon which I could draw as I offered guidance and support to this hurting congregation. Our desire was to offer the comfort of worship in the context of a reflective setting. We planned a service that would alternate Scripture readings and prayers from our new *Book of Common Worship* with moments of silent prayer and quiet organ music.

Meanwhile, the church was booming with activity despite the dreadful weather. Pastors from the presbytery had arrived, somber in mood, to offer pastoral care. Various church members had come to begin the phone calls, to bring food, to help the administrative staff. One minister from a neighboring presbytery came to offer condolences and assistance even though he lived 50 miles away. Bill Weber, a consultant to clergy and congregations through St. Vincent Hospital in Indianapolis, was also serving Northminster as a parish associate. (The position of parish associate is one available to presbytery clergy who serve in specialized ministries other than a parish. The relationship allows them to be part of the "extended" staff of a congregation without full-time service in that setting.) Because of his counseling background, Bill had the judgment to call the crisis response team at St. Vincent. After a brief discussion, we agreed that this team of Dr. Kay Schrader and Don Bare would remain on site for most of the day. Their availability proved invaluable to the staff and all others present.

Meeting with the administrative and program staff was the day's next demand. Again, we went over all the information we had and began to plan for the immediate work ahead. We quickly discussed the week's anticipated demands. There would be much to do—preparing for the evening's prayer service, arranging travel and accommodations for the Mathias family, and facing the challenge of the memorial service, which would likely be very large, given the size of the congregation and the effect of the murders on the entire community of Indianapolis.

We then held the first of many conferences with the staff to prepare for the deluge of "tough stuff." We talked about safety issues. How could they feel secure in the building? How should they handle telephone calls, including crank calls or so-called tips which inevitably come at such a time? Rightly anticipating that many offers of help would come directly to the church, we planned a strategy to respond. We identified an elder willing to keep track of all gifts, flowers, and other expressions of sympathy so that they could later be acknowledged. We discussed the presence of the police in the building and let the staff know that everyone would likely be interviewed at some point. The entire staff rallied to the church's needs in a remarkable way. Every staff member was in pain but able to function effectively under the growing pressure of the situation. There would be time for personal grief later.

Around 2:00 P.M. we agreed that the pastoral staff and I needed to rest before the prayer service. We had been going nonstop for 12 hours. We left in shifts so that one of us would always remain at the church. None of us got much sleep, although the quiet helped us prepare for the evening.

About 300 people, including the mayor and many pastors from the community, attended the prayer service, despite the inclement weather. Each of the worship leaders was positioned at a different door following the service so that we could speak with worshippers as they left. Many members remained in the church afterward, comforting one another.

Around 9:00 P.M. the chief investigating officer of the Marion County Homicide Unit arrived to take a statement from associate pastor Donna Wells, who was believed to have been the last person, other than the assailants, to see the victims alive. With the permission of the officers, I was present for the interview to offer emotional support. The complexity of our situation became more apparent as we realized that this would be only the first of many meetings with representatives of law-enforcement agencies. Although we had already made some decisions about increased security at the church, this interview offered another opportunity to discuss what precautions might be helpful, given the nature of the crime. The officers assured us as best they could that there was no reason to believe anyone else was in danger. This reassurance was only marginally comforting.

Tuesday morning held a number of demands as we began the long processional toward the Thursday morning memorial service. I was at the church by 8:00 A.M., anticipating another 14-hour day. The morning's first task was the "debriefing" of the staff by Kay Schrader from the St. Vincent crisis intervention team. In a total staff gathering, Dr. Schrader began with those who had been at the crime scene and pro-gressed through each staff member. We talked initially about the effect of stress on each of us and the importance of self-care during the tough hours ahead. We then heard from a Marion County sheriff's deputy, who dis-cussed safety in the building and addressed the staff's fears.

Looking back, I see that the numbness that frequently accompanies shock helped carry us through those first few days. Having at least noted the emotional and physical needs we were having, we could begin list-ing all the items that would need attention. The family would arrive on Wednesday afternoon; two hours of "calling" at the church were sched-uled for Wednesday evening. The steps to organize this visitation time —who would assist, which pastors would be present, and the like—were identified and assigned. Then we looked ahead to the memorial service. How many service bulletins should be prepared? Where would we get additional folding chairs? Who would "manage" the flowers? Funeral home staff had called to say they did not have enough stands for all the arrangements. What needs might the family have? Where would we arrange for overflow seating?

After the staff meeting, the pastors and I met to begin planning the memorial service. The family had asked us to make all the plans; their grief was too raw for such decisions. We considered two options. One would involve many speakers who had known the victims, including "dignitaries" who would surely be present. The other was to approach the service as we had the prayer gathering on Monday evening—as a worship service primarily for the family, congregation, and friends of the Mathiases. We chose the latter, and I believe it was the wiser path. It was agreed that Don Durrett would preach, given his long tenure at the church and the ministry of pastoral care he had extended to many members. Donna Wells would give the memorial moment for Mrs. Mathias, and I would give the one remembering Dr. Mathias.

Already a lump the size of a grapefruit was forming in my throat. Surely God would give us all the strength to get through this service. Music was carefully selected to make the service a celebration of life and a witness to the resurrection. This decision was an important part of the strategy suggested by the pastoral staff and affirmed by the session. We would use this tragedy to witness to the larger community so that all

would know we believed in the promises of God. Using the Presbyterian
Book of Common Worship, we planned a liturgy that would reflect our
beliefs and comfort those gathered. The service would last about one
hour. Later in the day the police conducted more interviews with staff.
During one of these we were told in confidence of the possibility that a
member of the church had been involved in the crimes. Our hearts sank,
but we began talking about how to handle such an eventuality.

Elder Mark Moore, spokesperson to the media, held the first of
several press conferences on Tuesday. He informed the press of the session's decision to allow television cameras in the sanctuary with certain
restrictions.

Wednesday was a blur, full of preparation for the calling that evening. By now, messages and expressions of sympathy were coming in
from all over the country. National network news had taken note of the
murders, and Mark Moore had been interviewed by National Public
Radio. The telephone rang constantly, sometimes with the expected
"tip" calls. Volunteers to answer the phones had been carefully selected
and trained to receive and refer such comments. Decisions on security
were being made. The Marion County Sheriff's Department would provide officers for both the visitation that evening and for the memorial
service Thursday. Thanks to the efforts of member David Donaldson and
the generosity of Comcast Cablevision of Indianapolis, the overflow
crowd in the fellowship hall would attend the service via closed-circuit
TV.

Other congregations rallied to the support of Northminster. The
youth group of Irvington Presbyterian Church provided child care for the
visitation. Second Presbyterian Church provided 200 folding chairs for
the service and volunteered its larger sanctuary, should the session wish
to hold the service there.

The arrival of the family was a time of high emotion. It was agreed
that the calling would take place in the sanctuary with the family present at the front. Stools were provided for them, should they tire during
the long visitation period. Funeral home representatives managed the
evening efficiently, especially the crowd flow. The pastors and I were
visible in the sanctuary where we could be found easily by mourners
who wished to speak with us. Information on memorial gifts was available in the narthex, as well as leaflets on dealing with trauma in children.

Thursday morning came all too soon. This was the first morning I did not arrive at the church by 8:00, choosing instead to continue working on my portion of the service at home. When I drove into the parking lot at 9:30 for the 11:00 A.M. memorial service, the lot was almost full. The service was a remarkable example of God's power to uplift and support God's people. More than a thousand people filled the church with song, prayer, and praise. Even the callous representatives of the media were touched, and one was heard to say, "This was a real surprise. It was a celebration of two lives, not at all like the funeral I expected!" This is not to say that grief went unacknowledged or that the senselessness of the act was ignored. Nothing pointed to this recognition as dramatically as the Scottish bagpiper who closed the service with "Amazing Grace." As he played, he walked slowly down the main aisle of the sanctuary, offering a grim reminder that the pastoral shepherd of this flock would walk it no more. Yet the intended message—that we believe God is in charge even amid such horror—came through loud and clear. All the television and newspaper accounts reflected the faith of this deeply wounded community. Even in death, Fred and Cleta Mathias were able to touch many others with the hope of the gospel.

First Baptist Church, Shelbyville, Indiana

When the pastor is a victim, mourning is clear-cut and understandable. But what happens when the mourning of a pastor is confused by whether the victim is really the pastor, the church, or both? That was the tragic question faced by First Baptist Church of Shelbyville, Indiana.

On the wall of the pastoral study of First Baptist was a poster of a brightly clad skier taking a gigantic leap off a snow-covered slope. The caption read, "Enthusiasm is Half the Journey!" Most people who knew the Rev. Martin Travelstead II said that enthusiasm was something he had in abundance. Marty was truly a "golden boy" with little experience in failure. He had served as an associate in two previous ministries and had one successful solo pastorate behind him. It was no surprise to others in the area when Marty was called to help First Baptist Church in Shelbyville deal with the challenges of its future.

This typical midwestern small-town congregation had an amazing growth record, going from eighty members to 240 members in eight years. The downside of increased membership was the difficult decision between relocating to a larger facility versus remodeling and enlarging the current downtown space. The former pastor was unable to resolve the deadlock, and eventually he resigned. At this point Marty Travelstead became head of staff. Everyone believed that Marty could help the congregation. But after five votes in two years, with relocation defeated by a narrow margin each time, Marty was feeling the stress of no definitive action. A strong stay/leave polarity in the congregation drained Marty's energy and seemingly left him feeling depressed and inadequate—perhaps for the first time in his career.

Shortly before the crisis events, Marty played golf with Riley Walker, Southwest area minister of the American Baptist Churches of Indiana. As Marty reflected on the troubling situation at the church, Riley suggested a new option. Why not have the best of both? Perhaps it was time to consider keeping the downtown site while organizing a satellite ministry on the growing outskirts of the community. Marty liked the idea and said he'd like to present it to his key leaders. There was no warning sign in this upbeat conversation that Marty was deeply troubled or unusually depressed. Riley left the golf course feeling good about the potential for First Church, and certainly for its star pastor, Marty Travelstead.

On Monday, May 19, 1997, Marty went to his office and lit a candle on a stack of papers resting on a shelf. He closed his door and left to drive to Indianapolis for a meeting. Since the church was across the street from the fire department, he was aware that the trucks were being serviced that day at the other fire station and hence not readily available to the church facility. Who can guess what Marty was thinking as he drove away from the congregation he loved so much? We only know that he soon received a call on his cellular phone: "The church building is on fire!" Marty turned around and rushed back to the scene, where raging flames were taking their toll on a building that some viewed as an asset and others as a roadblock. Later, it was learned that Marty had considred starting a fire before but, in his own words, "couldn't do it." He had obviously become more and more despondent in the last week.

That evening a nearby Presbyterian church opened its doors so that First Baptist could have a worship service and gathering for the community. Marty chose Psalm 63, one of his favorites, as the text for the evening. Looking back later, some members of the congregation wondered what Marty was trying to say, especially with the last verse, which reads, "for the mouths of liars will be stopped." Marty had repeatedly denied his involvement in the fire. Was this his confession? Pastor Marty Travelstead was in his own personal wilderness.

Tuesday morning made the reality of the fire and its aftermath hard to forget. Marty learned that after the torching of so many African-American churches in the South, it was now standard practice for the Justice Department to deploy the Bureau of Alcohol, Tobacco, and Firearms to investigate church fires. Marty, upset with this unexpected twist, called Riley Walker, saying, "Riley, they're going to pin this on me." Riley thought Marty's concern was having been the last person in the church building before the fire. He counseled Marty to stick to the truth to ensure that there would be no problems for him. After a breakfast meeting the morning after the fire, Marty also shared his fears with Capt. Mark Mason of the Indiana State Police. Mark was chairman of the board of trustees at First Baptist and a close friend. Mark realized that Marty was deeply disturbed and asked him if he'd set the fire. Marty was unable to admit the truth, even to a man with whom he had prayed often and shared his personal and professional life.

Marty had lunch with a friend between noon and one and then drove to his parents' home in Brown County near the town of Nashville, Indiana. An outdoorsman who loved hiking in the woods of the local state park, Marty felt closest to God in Brown County. It was, for him, holy ground. Finding his parents away, Marty went into the house, where he typed two notes on the computer. In one note he admitted setting the fire and described the events of several days earlier. A second, more personal note was addressed to his family and the church. He asked for forgiveness. Marty then took one of his father's guns, walked to a ravine at the back of the family property, and ended his life.

When Marty did not return home that afternoon, his wife, Carol, knew something was terribly wrong. It was unlike Marty simply to disappear. Carol called Mark Mason. If anything had happened, surely Mark would know. But Mark had heard nothing. About an hour later Carol received a call from Marty's parents. His car had been found behind the barn. Mark rushed to Carol's side and drove her to Brown County. They heard the heartbreaking news of Marty's suicide when they arrived.

News travels fast in small towns. As word leaked out, many community pastors and members of First Baptist began to gather in the fellowship hall. Tom Bartley, the associate pastor, called a deacon and trustee meeting for 10:00 that evening. Riley Walker, who had already been called, arrived at the church almost immediately after learning of the suicide.

Just as at the meeting of Northminster's session, the church leaders were first given accurate information. After opening with prayer, Tom told the story, and they began to deal with immediate needs. How should they care for Carol and the children? What should be their response to Marty's parents?

Finally, the leaders planned an initial care strategy for the congregation, which included disseminating accurate information and making pastoral care available to individuals having significant emotional difficulty. The membership roll was divided among the deacons present, and every family in the church was called. The evening was closed with the Lord's Prayer.

The next day, Patrick Travelstead asked his mother if he could go to school. Carol, having thought she would keep him home with the family, agreed because his normal routine appeared to give Patrick stability. The boy had not yet been told the nature of his father's death, only that he'd been shot. One of the worst moments in this tragedy occurred when Patrick learned that his father's death had been a suicide. He was asked about it by middle-school students who had heard it that morning over their school's public address system. A fifth-grader, Patrick was visiting their school that day.

That evening two meetings were held—one for members of First Baptist and a prayer meeting sponsored by a neighboring congregation. At both meetings the county prosecutor and members of the local fire department and the Federal Bureau of Alcohol, Tobacco, and Firearms were present to give accounts of what had happened in the building. The purpose was to dispel rumors, convey accurate information, and lend support to one another. About 250 people attended.

The open meeting for the congregation consisted of approximately 20 small groups facilitated by the American Baptist clergy and community health workers from Gallahue Mental Health Center. Two groups were provided for children and one for adolescents. In these small groups the story was repeated once again. This account reinforced the first telling and ensured that everyone heard it correctly. People were invited to respond as they felt led to do so. Individuals who were not coping well were referred to deacons after the meeting for follow-up care. The Lord's Prayer became the unifying theme at the close of this evening, as it had been for the deacons the night before.

Carol Travelstead made the funeral plans in consultation with the associate pastor. Carol boldly stated, "This is the last date with the man I love, and I want it to be a celebration." The service included remarks by several speakers, some of whom acknowledged that although what Martin had done was difficult to understand, he would still be loved and missed. Marty's good friend John Parsley of First Baptist Church in Plainfield, Indiana, preached the message, which focused on a celebration of life and offered support to the family. Other churches and the wider community rallied to support the Travelstead family and the First Baptist congregation by attending this important service.

Riley Walker says he believes that this tragedy illustrates a serious problem among church professionals. The journey of Marty Travelstead points us all to the dark side of clergy stress and burnout. In an interview with me six months later Riley reflected, "On the macro scale Marty was the least likely of American Baptist clergy to have done this. He had all the resources but didn't use them. On the micro scale, it is understandable in retrospect. He felt he'd personally failed the church and God. He just couldn't forgive himself." For Marty, in the end, the enthusiasm noted on his office poster just wasn't enough.

Oklahoma City and the Murrah Building Bombing

Michael Fletcher-Taylor—co-pastor with his wife, Sharon, of Mayfair Heights United Methodist Church in Oklahoma City—was sitting at his desk at 9:02 A.M. on April 19, 1995. When he felt a tremor and objects began to fall off his shelf, he knew something had happened. Jumping into his truck, Michael saw clouds of smoke billowing from the downtown area seven miles away. He assumed there had been a gas explosion.

Margaret Ball, a former chaplain at Baptist Medical Center, was in the underground level of the Church of the Servant talking on the phone when she felt the ground shake under her. Assuming that there had been an explosion in her building, she quickly ended the call and rushed to the hallway. Seeing no damage, she assumed she'd heard a sonic boom. Margaret was 15 miles from the center of the city.

P. G. Legg, a Methodist laywoman, was only five blocks away from the Alfred P. Murrah Federal Building when hell visited Oklahoma City. Her office lights began to flicker, the building swayed violently, and people rushed to the street, where they saw a mushroom cloud of smoke rising upward. The sight brought to mind photographs of Hiroshima.

The question "Where were you when . . ." is not new to the American public. People who recall the early 1940s associate it with learning of the attack on Pearl Harbor. Those with memories of the 1960s think of the assassination of John F. Kennedy. Young and old alike will raise this question in years to come as we remember the terrible act of violence perpetrated on innocent children, employees, and visitors who were in the Murrah Building on April 19, 1995, when a terrorist bomb blast devastated the nine-story office complex.

The world stood still for the people of Oklahoma City and for the nation on that crisp spring morning. We remained mesmerized by the media for weeks following the tragic bombing, hoping for answers to the horrible questions "Why?" "Who?" and "How many?" We watched the reports of deaths and injuries mount to the final toll of 149 adults and 19 children killed. In a split second our world was permanently changed. Our fragile trust that "it couldn't happen here" was lost for all time. It had happened, and the Church of Jesus Christ was there in its midst. Michael, P. G., and Margaret were only a few of the courageous and faithful pastors and laypeople I interviewed for this book. Through their stories I hope readers can learn more about the witness of the church to the world when trauma envelops a whole community.

Robert Allen, senior minister of St. Luke's United Methodist Church, a downtown congregation, had attended a meeting with Ron Norick, mayor of Oklahoma City, the morning before the bombing. When the crisis hit, the mayor remembered meeting Bob and asked him if he'd coordinate the clergy volunteers needed to respond. Through Bob's immediate response, clergy began to pour into the area within the hour. In the hours after the tragedy the trauma manifested itself in understandable chaos. Volunteers could walk very close to the site. The tight security checks that would be imposed later were not yet in place. Arriving clergy were given name tags that Bob had typed out on his computer. He'd been selective in calling those whom he knew to be mature in faith and able to bear the burden of caring for others in extreme circumstances.

Around 11:00 A.M. Mike and Sharon Fletcher-Taylor arrived in the area and were assigned to work with Team One. Joining them was Tish McLoy, a Methodist pastor who had been a chaplain in Kansas City when a balcony in the Hyatt Regency Hotel collapsed. They learned that there were fatalities in the federal building's day-care center, and were asked to go there. The team received no prior coaching. Its members were told to "go be pastors." In her hurry to help, Sharon had not thought to change her shoes. She began to walk through the rubble in high-heeled dress pumps. Mike described the scene as "like a war zone —glass, smoke, debris." Children's bodies were being laid out on the street in front of the damaged First United Methodist Church, which was quickly becoming a makeshift morgue. As chaos drifted into order, Mike and Sharon were among a few clergy asked to remain in the "pit," the name given to the collapsed area through which workers were searching for survivors. They worked evening shifts and continued to provide a ministry of presence. Volunteers at Mayfield United Methodist Church filled in on the maintenance of parish life during the next 14 days.

Margaret Ball served in the pit too, until she was moved to the Family Assistance Center set up at First Christian Church, where her prior experience with grieving families was greatly needed. Margaret met me for our interview with a yellow hard hat in her hand. A crude stick cross had been drawn on it with a black Magic Marker. The letters beneath it said "CLERGY." Margaret and her colleagues wore this headgear as they walked among the workers. She told of one emotionally shaken worker who had been excavating remains, to whom she reached out her hand. "Don't touch me," he said. "I can't do this if I think about it."

A team of three chaplains would be called whenever a body was removed. It was always a "holy moment." Silence would descend on the otherwise noisy scene, and hard hats would come off. One moving moment came when a piece of bright red cloth was seen in the gray concrete landscape. As it was uncovered, workers realized it was the American flag. It was quietly and reverently hoisted on the arm of a bulldozer to fly amid the rescue efforts and a vale of tears.

As the days dragged on and the weather changed from cool to hot, volunteers began to drift away. A few chaplains remained for the entire two weeks. Some days were dull; they simply stood around. When it became apparent that most of the bodies had been removed, the relief workers sought out the chaplains less often. But still the clergy stayed. Most of their time was spent talking with the military troops, police guards, and construction workers. After this exhausting term of service Michael Fletcher-Taylor didn't return to the site for over a year. When he did, it was to accompany a confirmation class that wanted to visit the chapel erected on the morgue site. When I asked Mike how his pastoral experience at the disaster site had shaped his faith, he reflected, "I always knew who God was, but this experience has made me more aware of who I am to be."

LeRoy Thompson was also a bomb site volunteer. Because of his past position as director of behavioral medicine at Presbyterian Hospital, he had been called to be part of a trauma team. LeRoy reminded me that the best workers were those who had no ego investment, had no need of recognition, and came on site not out of curiosity but with a desire to help. He described the work of pastors in the pit as a ministry of presence, not of words. These courageous clergy were called upon to serve in ways for which they could have never prepared.

Gale Izard, a retired army reserve chaplain, thought he had seen it all. Seeing a morgue just for babies pushed the limits of what even he could handle. Gale was speaking from the depth of his heartbreak when he told me, "Serving in that morgue destroyed my assumption that I can fix it." Protestant ministers were asked to assist in giving the last rites of the church to those who may have been Catholic, since there were not enough priests to serve each shift. One pastor's job was to call an emotionally shaky relief worker who, having finished a 12-hour shift, had gone to his motel room alone. His buddies were worried about him. Another chaplain simply sat quietly beside a construction worker as he held a teddy bear and cried. LeRoy said, "We did not go with our own power, but only by God's power."

Steve Vinson, director of the United Methodist Church Circle of Care, described his work at the bomb site as a "ministry of wandering around." That description cannot begin to explain the service he rendered during those harrowing two weeks. Steve was asked by Robert Allen to coordinate the clergy volunteers. Upon his arrival, he stepped into the mix of Red Cross workers, social services staff, therapists, and various federal and military staff on the scene.

In addition to working the six-to-midnight shift, Steve determined what "clearance" each volunteer received. The FBI had established a color-coding system that allowed access to particular areas. Steve's yellow badge gave him almost unlimited freedom to move from place to place. The decision to grant or limit access was often taxing and was, in the end, a judgment call. When a Native American pastor with few credentials presented himself to Steve as a "tribal traditionalist," Steve decided to grant him access because he knew there were Native American victims as well as construction and relief workers of Native American heritage. A different call was made when a minister with some public recognition from outside the community appeared with a camera crew in tow. Access was denied because of the questionable goals of the visit.

In the first days after the tragedy Steve found himself directing food vendors, working at the command post of the military to help stock the pharmacy established for relief workers, or loading wheelbarrows with bottles of water, snacks, and other things that could be rolled by chaplains to those on site. Steve discovered the art of asking questions based on quick impressions of a person's appearance. To some he'd say, "Boy, this rain is really the pits," to start a conversation. To weary workers needing a cheerful word he might call out, "Welcome to McDonald's. May I take your order?" His tender presence and his talent of matching the dialogue to the person made him a much-beloved figure in the weeks that followed.

Some of the most moving accounts of those days also came from Steve. He reported how the average person often rallied to the challenge of loving one's neighbor. He was listening to the radio at the command post when a call went out over the airwaves that excavation workers needed steel-toed boots. Very quickly a beat-up pickup truck drove to the makeshift fence erected for security. When Steve was motioned over, he saw an older man whose face showed the toll of hard work. The man stuck a pair of still-warm boots out the window for Steve to take— and drove away barefoot. On another day Steve commented to a guard, "Who is that lady over there?" referring to an elderly woman sitting in a van. The woman, who had appeared several days in a row, was hooked up to a portable oxygen system. "Oh, that's the laundry lady," the guard replied. "She comes every day and takes home any dirty clothes that workers need washing." Steve reminded me that the destruction of the Murrah Building was an incredible act of cowardice that brought out the very best in human beings.

Ministry in the pit and the surrounding area was emotionally draining and psychologically difficult. The sights, sounds, and smells of those
days will endure for a lifetime in the minds of those who served. Preparation and debriefing were attempted for each six-hour shift, but often
the hectic demands of the service kept everyone from attending. The
bombing site was not the only place of taxing service. Some clergy took
on the draining task of ministering to the families waiting to hear if their
loved one was among the living or the dead.

On the day of the bombing Delbert Hamm, a retired Christian
Church (Disciples of Christ) pastor, was serving as a part-time interim
associate pastor at First Christian Church. Driving toward town from an
auto repair shop in Midwest City, Del saw the smoke cloud blocking the
downtown skyline. Little did he know that his church would soon
become the host building for the family assistance center. Don Alexander,
First Christian's senior minister, had contacted the American Red Cross,
offering the church's facilities for whatever was needed. Within 45
minutes the Oklahoma Funeral Directors Association had responded to
the invitation. Initially, the hope was to use the church as an information
center. Several months earlier the funeral directors' group had designed
a disaster plan. It called for a place easily secured, accessible to inter-
state travel, and near the incident site. First Christian met all these criteria and quickly became the family assistance center, the base of opera-
tions for a number of service agencies.

In the next few days the church staff worked alongside 150 volunteers from the congregation plus many others to make the church a
haven for those waiting to hear about loved ones. Del helped coordinate
building use. With the help of the American Red Cross, the Salvation
Army, and almost every other social-service agency in the city, the
church building was transformed into a service area. People arrived in
droves, carrying with them dental records, birth certificates, handprints
forming the front of a Mother's Day card—anything that could help
identify a victim.

The dining room was set up with tables for families. The kitchen
prepared and served three meals a day from food donated by restaurants
and distributors for the three weeks that the assistance center remained
in operation. The Jewel Box Community Theater was set up as a media
center where the press and others could obtain screened access to interviews. Forty phone lines were installed by Southwestern Bell so that the

waiting families could have unlimited telephone time with family and friends across the country. Once a day the medical examiner, the fire chief, and the chief of police would meet with the families for a briefing on the rescue and recovery efforts.

The church's main floor became the command center, which was basically under Pentagon control. It was here that the work of the medical examiners, funeral directors, social workers, and others was coordinated. The facility was secured by the National Guard with protected entrances and exits. The third floor became a trauma center with medical staff readily available to serve family members who needed medication or other treatment. The fourth floor was available to medical examiners.

Whenever word reached the command post that the remains of a victim had been positively identified, the family would be escorted to the fourth floor by a chaplain and, when applicable, by an official from the agency related to the deceased, such as the Social Security Administration. There family members were officially informed by medical examiners of the verification of death. They were then escorted out a private and secure exit door unknown to the public.

In the long days of waiting, the church allowed "therapy animals" to be brought into the building. Dogs, rabbits, and a monkey named Charlie helped adults and children to cope with the uncertainty and brought a sense of comfort. One little boy, waiting to hear about the fate of a parent, broke out in his first and only smile when Charlie hopped over to him.

Del Hamm reported that the church's ministry grew during those days. On the second floor the daily preschool continued, the teachers and parents willingly living with the limits of using only one entrance-way. The parking lot was roped off to half its size for Sunday worship parking. As members and pastors pitched in to offer the hospitality of Christ during the darkest moments, they found themselves spiritually blessed. "It was amazing to see a retired millionaire sweeping the floors," Del reflected. "We all learned about servanthood."

Most of us knew of the loss of 169 lives in the Oklahoma City bombing. Few of us realized that more than 600 injuries occurred as the impact of the explosion blew out plate-glass windows within a 20-block radius, hurling glass and flying debris toward the unsuspecting bystanders. In addition, 462 people were left homeless, many of them limited- and lower-income individuals dependent on low-rent housing near the bombing site. Eighteen blocks were affected in the downtown business district, where 16,000 people were employed. Seven thousand of these workers were now displaced. Again, the church was there, ready to serve.

Dave Poteet, along with the senior minister of St. Luke's United Methodist Church, Robert Long, was proud of the ministry to the displaced rendered by the congregation after the bombing. The initial site for family assistance, St. Luke's took over the enormous job of coordinating shelter, food, and clothing for the low-income homeless. From 200 to 300 people were provided places to sleep, and over 1,000 meals a day were served. The public's generosity was so great that there was always more food than needed. Because Dave was heard in a CNN television interview, his name became associated nationwide with relief efforts. At one point he was walking around with more than $5,000 in his pocket, just from donations handed through the fence. Dave said the most important lesson for him was a new appreciation for the fragility of life. We need to use our time here well, he added.

Dene Brown, director of Skyline Urban Ministry, an outreach to the city through the Oklahoma Annual Conference of the United Methodist Church, explained to me further ramifications for the people who had lived in the area affected by the bombing. People who were paying $150 a month for low-rent housing later learned that if and when their buildings were reconstructed, the new residences would target a high-end market. As secondary victims of this tragedy, these city-dwellers were being pushed farther and farther from the services they depended upon for survival. People who used to walk four blocks to Skyline's ministry programs would have to come a mile or more to reach these services.

Yet come they did! The "A" Street program, "Alive on Saturday Night," usually attracted between 40 and 50 participants. In the weeks following the bombing, it drew up to 200. Those affected needed a place to be together and to experience God's promise of hope. One man from the streets appeared in tears—he had lost his only friend in the world, a Social Security Administration employee had who greeted him each morning on the way to an office in the Murrah Building. In response to the overwhelming needs of survivors and families of victims, the United Methodist conference asked Dene Brown to hire someone to

manage a program to assist them. Dene knew just who could do the job
—P. G. Legg.

P. G. Legg knew many people who worked in the Murrah Building.
She had recruited them to adopt inner-city families for the holiday
season each year. An African-American woman, P. G. related well to
the racially diverse population she sought to serve. For three years after
the bombing, her ministry involved serving on a variety of boards and
projects that funded relief and post-trauma services. She became well
versed in the work of the Federal Emergency Management Agency,
emergency services from denominational disaster plans, the American
Red Cross, and others. In a city struggling to manage the millions of
relief dollars pouring in, P. G. became known as a true advocate for
survivors and victims' families. She worked extensively doing case
intakes for her own ministry through Skyline and for other agencies as
well. Of all the lives she touched, none were more special than the 30
children who were orphaned and the 219 who lost at least one parent.
She was a voice, and a strong one, on their behalf. A later chapter will
discuss P. G.'s work, along with that of Tracey Evans, who held a
similar position with the Presbytery of Indian Nations, in "Safe Haven,"
an ecumenical program that provided support, respite, and hospitality
during the trials of accused bombers Timothy McVeigh and Terry
Nichols.

The ecumenical and interfaith communities joined hands during the
recovery period. Among the groups formed was the Interfaith Disaster
Recovery of Greater Oklahoma City, Inc. Dr. Rita Newton Cowan, who
became the director of the Oklahoma Council of Churches after the
bombing, was involved in the work of this organization, which hired a
director and a case manager to assist in the distribution of relief funds.
The council of churches played a pastoral role and worked to assist
judicatories and other organizations in fulfilling their ministries. Judicatory leaders were convened by the council periodically for information sharing and support.

Dr. John Russo thinks a lot about how this tragedy has affected the
city he's served for many years. As dean of the Chapel at Oklahoma
City University and an adjunct professor in the Wimberly School of
Religion, he has also taught in the Department of Counseling Psychology.
In the initial days following the bombing, John was involved in the
many religious services and counseling situations that one would expect

following a great trauma. Another contribution, however, has been his reflections on the continuing impact of an act of violence on the community and on the lives of individuals. Three weeks after the bombing, John led a day for area clergy titled, "What Do I Say on Mother's Day?" Helping clergy in the community to rethink their theology in light of what had happened was no easy task. John observed the effects of trauma in his role as pastoral counselor, taking special note of Vietnam veterans who were retraumatized by the bombing.

Although Oklahoma City had no looting incidents in the aftermath of the bombing (despite the fact that cash drawers at a local bank were left open and unsecured for more than a week), John observed other signs of distress in the community. Expressions of rage, bar fights, and weapons incidents were all on the increase in the months immediately following. Influenced by the thinking of Carl Jung, John believes that Evil surfaced on April 19, 1995, and that this shadow will remain in our corporate memories for a long, long time. From a three-year distance, I think he's right.

The face of trauma has many guises. Murder, suicide, arson, and bombing only scratch the surface of how the lives of individuals, congregations, and communities can be affected. I am grateful to all those who told the stories related here. Perhaps putting faces and names on trauma will help us understand the importance of the church's ministry to those touched by traumatic events.

CHAPTER 4

When the Trauma Is Disaster

How can we rebuild? How can we ever hope to have a place where battered bodies and spirits can live secure, hopeful, proud again? Having fun, taking a vacation, telling a joke, and sleeping in the sun seems as impossible as sprouting wings. What is left in the rubble of naïveté and trust, yes, even in you, God, that can be used to start over?

—Margaret Anne Huffman,
"Through the Valley..." Prayers for Violent Times, p. 126

Any trauma feels like a disaster to the ones most directly affected. The United Methodist Committee on Relief defines disaster as "a rolling series of disruptions of personal and community life involving a significant number of people, causing spiritual, emotional, physical and social crises to which the Church responds with God's love and help."[1] Disasters can be part of the natural world—earthquakes, floods, tornadoes—or can be the result of human intent, error, or accident as in toxic spills, nuclear accidents, bombings, or civil unrest. Disasters usually affect large numbers of people and institutions, including churches. It is helpful for leaders of congregations to have some knowledge of disaster response, what people need in times of crisis, and the emotional impact when their church is directly affected by the disaster. When disaster strikes, trained individuals will generally be present to shepherd pastors and congregations through the maze of response and relief.

Four general stages follow every disaster:

1. *The emergency stage.* This period begins when disaster strikes and continues until all affected people have been found or accounted for. The work to be done involves serving immediate needs for shelter, food, and clothing, as well as emergency medical care. The state civil-preparedness arm of government protects life and property during this time. The American Red Cross and the Salvation Army are almost always first on the scene. Many local people and agencies, including churches, are involved in responding to immediate need.

2. *The relief stage.* The American Red Cross works with other agencies to develop assistance centers and to continue providing for human need. Groups of people begin to come forward to help with clean-up or repair. If the state governor has obtained a full presidential declaration of disaster, the Federal Emergency Management Agency (FEMA) will begin granting federal assistance to disaster survivors.

3. *The disillusionment stage.* Residents initially react with euphoria over the amount of help coming into the area. Money, clothing, and food are donated from all over the country. As reality sets in, however, many begin to feel a loss of personal control. The dollars are allocated in specific ways. People who have never before needed to ask for help are embarrassed or feel a loss of dignity in asking for it now. Bewildering numbers of agencies and groups offer what seem to be duplicate services. Finding the right people to respond to questions may be difficult.

4. *The recovery stage.* This period can last several years beyond the disaster as media attention, financial support, and volunteer efforts gradually wane. Finding the energy needed to continue rebuilding the community and the lives of those affected is often a challenge.[2] This decline in public attention was made clear to me when someone learning of my trip to Oklahoma City commented, "What is Jill doing in Oklahoma City? That bombing happened three years ago." Most people do not realize how long true recovery can take.

The church's response to disaster will be most effective if thought about in two phases. The first phase is the relief of suffering and need. The second is the long-term recovery of the community. The United Methodist Church is among the denominations having a well-conceived plan for the long-term care needed by many.

What People Need When Disaster Strikes

People have emotional needs in addition to their need for information about recovery and assistance after a major calamity. Many of these dynamics are present in all traumas, but they are especially relevant when the tragedy is beyond human action. Pastors and caregivers should be aware that people need:

1. To talk about what happened and what it means for them.

2. To distinguish clearly between what happened and what they wish had happened.

3. To name feelings, positive and negative, and to know these feelings to be legitimate.

4. To receive accurate information about what happened and what will happen.

5. To relate this tragedy to other events and times in their lives.

6. To explain to themselves what has happened so they can believe it is real.

7. To remember what they did to feel better in other situations of loss or to hear what others may be doing to help themselves feel better.

Remember that the initial response to disaster is highly reactive and involves attending to the immediate needs of assessing damage, finding shelter when needed, and attending to the basic requirements of life. The concerns listed above often do not surface until the immediate response period is over.

Agencies to the Rescue

It is important that we understand the nature of the partnerships that link our congregation, our denomination, ecumenical relief organizations, and community agencies that work together when disaster strikes. When the community of faith gathers its resources and works cooperatively to respond to disaster, the witness is truly remarkable. Most individuals participate in disaster relief with financial gifts channeled through their worshipping community or the American Red Cross.

By congressional charter on January 5, 1905, the American Red Cross was designated the nationwide agency through which the American people voluntarily extend assistance to those in need when disaster hits. The Red Cross often manages the major thrust of emergency and relief effort in a community in partnership with other major organizations. The agency divides the United States into three operational jurisdictions with an administrative and field staff located in each. Most mainline denominations join the Red Cross in one of two ways, through a partnership with Church World Service or through an agency of the denomination organized specifically for relief response efforts.

Organized in 1946, Church World Service (CWS) is the disaster-relief, refugee, and development unit of the National Council of the Churches of Christ in the U.S.A. The CWS Emergency Response office strives to have an ecumenical disaster readiness-and-response representative in each state. When disaster strikes, these trained disaster-resource consultants assist the faith community in organizing a coordinated response to the situation. Some denominations—the Presbyterian Church (U.S.A.), the United Church of Christ, the Episcopal Church, and the Christian Church (Disciples of Christ)— approach disaster response as a program of the national denomination implemented by denominational staff and resources, often in partnership with CWS.

A second way the Christian community has responded to disaster has been to organize separate denominational agencies capable of responding on their own but working in consultation and partnership with CWS. This has been the avenue taken by the United Methodists, Catholic Charities, Mennonites (through the Mennonite Central Committee), and the Evangelical Lutheran Church in America, among others. Naturally many other denominations and independent religious organizations have their own strategies for responding during these crises. The Salvation Army is always a key organization in offering help. There are many disaster-relief tables with different partners sitting at each. To learn more about a denomination's program on the Internet, link through the Church World Service web page (nccusa.org/cws), or go directly to the denomination's home page on the web.

When the Church Building Is Affected

One of the most challenging aspects of recovery from disaster is the damage or destruction of church property. Most of us intellectually know that the building is not the church, yet it still "houses" our image of the sacred. If lives have been lost as a result of the building's being damaged, the first response is always concern and support for the grieving survivors or those recovering from injuries. If no one is hurt or injured, attention shifts immediately to the lost worship center.

Remembering that individuals surviving disaster may have suffered multiple losses—home, place of employment, friends or relatives killed or injured—it is easy to understand how devastating the loss of the church building can be. It is one more layer of grief, this time connected to a place that holds deep psychological and spiritual meaning for those who worship there.

Even when insurance coverage is adequate and denominational resources can assist in rebuilding, a deep sense of loss is experienced by most churchgoers. We cannot replace the sanctuary in which we were married, our children were baptized, and our husband was buried. Repairs may be delayed because of insurance disputes or other settlements. If the building has been destroyed, the pastor and congregational leaders may be emotionally unable to design a new building or to determine whether the time is right to relocate. All of these factors should be taken seriously by "outside" helpers such as judicatory executives seeking to assist.

Emotional Reactions to Disaster

A previous chapter dealt with emotional and psychological dimensions of trauma. Pastors and other caregivers should be aware of a few other aspects because of emotions that complicate the healing process. In the emergency stage of disaster people usually focus first on basic needs, then move toward a determination to bring order out of chaos. They work together with individuals with whom they would rarely come in contact under normal conditions. At times it seems that energy for the response is unending and the community pulls together as never before. Then, as the weeks and months creep by, people may begin feeling depressed, angry, and frustrated. Physical fatigue sets in. Information comes in distorted forms. No one seems to know what is working and what isn't.

A key milestone in climbing out of this valley seems to be reached when displaced people are able to return to their homes or when the assistance needed for repairs becomes available. As major life problems begin to be solved, individuals start moving from the lowest point upward in the cycle of healing. This recovery can take anywhere from ten months to a year to achieve. Those who were already struggling before the disaster have a harder time recovering, and sometimes the disaster is the last straw. The rate of divorce often rises following major disasters. As they offer pastoral care to families, pastors and other caregivers should be aware of the strain that calamities place on marriage.

Responding to Caregivers

In times of disaster the church may be called upon to offer support to caregivers who deal more directly with disaster victims. This need was cited in the case study of the Oklahoma City bombing. It is important to remember that medical workers, social workers, psychologists, public-school teachers, and many others in the community are affected because of their unique role as "helper." Official response programs will likely organize debriefings, but the pastor or counselor in a particular congregation may still have work uniquely cut out for him or her.

In cases of mass casualties another segment of the community will be in need of care—funeral directors and their employees. We sometimes think these men and women are not in need because they deal daily with the realities of death and destruction. How untrue! When funeral home management and staff deal with multiple deaths and the families connected to them, the stress can become almost unmanageable. Congregations can offer support through prayer and notes of support. When the immediate crisis is over, the clergy in a community can reverse the roles and take the funeral director to lunch. Looking for small ways to offer care will be effective in the recovery days ahead.

Judicatory staff members should be aware that the pastors of congregations in the affected area will be traumatized too. Consider bringing in a group of retired clergy or ministers serving outside the area in settings other than the parish to assist in pastoral care or preaching while the resident pastor recovers or deals with personal and family needs. Remember to follow up with pastors periodically through the year following the disaster.

Preparing for Disaster

When disaster strikes, the greater church is ready to respond. When we are directly affected by the disaster, it is better to receive the care of others than to attempt to do it all ourselves. There are, however, a few things we can do to feel more informed about and prepared for such difficult times.

1. Review the church's insurance coverage annually. This task is particularly important if the church is located in a flood plain or in an area where weather-related disasters are likely to occur.

2. Become familiar with the local chapter of the American Red Cross and other organizations in the community prepared to offer help.

3. Learn about the disaster plan for your community or county. Review the role of churches and religious organizations in it.

4. Inquire about the possibility of a local training program that might be sponsored through a ministerial association or council of churches to equip parish pastors for disaster response. Pastors completing the program could be given disaster identification badges for emergency use.

5. Consider a disaster interpretation program for your congregation. Sensitive information about the necessity of access to dental records, birth certificates, and other records could be discussed in a nonthreatening, supportive environment.

6. Identify categories of people in your community who might be in special need should a disaster occur.

7. When volunteering in disaster recovery, be aware of cultural differences. Understanding practices such as the custom of

addressing older adults as "Mr." or "Mrs." in the African-American community goes a long way in restoring the sense of "place" in the community.

With God's help the trauma of disaster can be managed. This is a time when the partnership of various religious groups unites us beyond our individual expressions and families of faith. Through the generosity and perseverance of congregations, pastors, denominations, and partner organizations, healing can take place.

CHAPTER 5

Strategies for Caring and Coping

We beg from our knees: Help us to rebuild. Give us a blueprint for recovery, a road map to healing. We are burning beneath the debris of others dumping. Hear us calling you from the filth. Find us. Help us to dig out. Be the foundation upon which we rebuild.

—Margaret Anne Huffman,
"Through the Valley..." Prayers for Violent Times, p. 126

The stories in chapter three of Northminster Presbyterian, First Baptist, and Oklahoma City reflect unique situations but many common themes. Who is most affected by this trauma? Where are the groups and individuals in this congregation who need the most immediate or long-term care? What about the surviving family members when there is a murder or suicide? What about those in the larger circle of impact—the presbytery, the diocese, the conference? How do any of us, really, ever get over such dreadful happenings—especially when they occur in the most sacred place of our life, our church?

This chapter is intended to give the reader a framework for addressing the needs of God's people in the long days of healing ahead. The suggestions include strategies for working with members of the church staff; key leadership groups, including the board/vestry/session or council; children, youth and their parents; and particular adult populations such as homebound members or individuals close to the tragedy. I will also explore care of the congregation as a whole through programs and resources designed to promote coping and healing.

Caring for the Family

In an interview with the author, Carol Travelstead, widow of the Baptist pastor who took his own life, confirmed the obvious: "I felt like everyone was watching me." The extraordinary scrutiny of family members in the public eye is almost indescribable. It is stressful enough when members of the media are constantly hounding the family; it is even more disturbing when well-meaning members of congregations add to the stress. The delicate balance of providing support without intruding on the private grief of family members is, indeed, an art. Since each situation is unique, it is difficult to identify common links. Special care and concern should be given to these families. Among the things to remember:

1. Make certain the family has accurate information.

In the Mathias murders the police were excellent in giving family members updates and details. Since the family lived in another state, I made it a point to send copies of newspaper articles from the Indianapolis papers to supplement the regular police reports. We also made certain that the family received periodic summaries of the cards, notes, and memorials that arrived at the church, and we offered to respond on their behalf. The hospitality offered by the congregation during the funeral and return trips to settle the estate continued the church's care of the family.

Carol Travelstead had a different experience. Because of the nature of her loss, it was often difficult for her to obtain accurate information. Individuals reluctant to add to her distress didn't offer many details. She often felt that she was left on her own to piece together what had happened.

In the Oklahoma City bombing, locating the care of families at the family assistance center was a key factor in the instant support provided by the community of faith. The pastors present as chaplains were often the families' only source of regular information during the first days after the bombing. Waiting with the families for information about their loved ones was a key pastoral task.

2. Respect the family's privacy.

The examples of First Baptist in Shelbyville and Northminster Presbyterian in Indianapolis provide different views of a family's needs. Carol Travelstead and her children were well known to the Shelbyville community and to members of the congregation. In contrast, Mark and Garth Mathias and their sister, Ann O'Neal, had visited Northminster occasionally but knew few people beyond the pastoral staff. Clearly, the response needed to be different.

A close friend volunteered to do "door duty" at the Travelstead home. When a visitor appeared, he or she was greeted at the door and asked to sign a calling sheet but to respect Carol's need for privacy. Gifts were graciously taken and acknowledged on the sign-in sheet. All arrangements for the Mathias family were made by the church, and volunteers were carefully selected to provide transportation and meals during their visit. The management of flowers, memorial gifts to the church, and other expressions of concern was delegated to one elder.

Churches can help by being aware of the family's specific needs. The culture of the community often shapes the response. For instance, bringing food to a bereaved family is customary in some regions. Yet the last thing a grieving family needs is the challenge of fitting 37 chicken casseroles into the freezer. A member of the church assigned to manage such generosities can be helpful. One scenario I studied included the thoughtful idea of donating perishable food that could not be used by the family to a homeless shelter. The church office should be aware of what is needed and when, to guide parishioners wanting to help. Sometimes the initial response is tremendous, leaving the long weeks ahead bereft of resources. Pacing support and care over a longer period of time may be of greatest benefit. When young children are involved, other items might be helpful. One basket left at the Travelstead home held a note which read, "I figured you had enough lasagna," and was full of "kid stuff" for the children. Who could have seen television during the days following the Oklahoma City tragedy without weeping over the number of teddy bears brought to the site? Such memorials were distributed to families and the surplus sent to children's homes and hospitals across the nation.

3. Remember to encourage appropriate messages to the families.

When parishioners turn to you with the fear, "I don't know what to say," encourage them not to say much. Most families interviewed agreed that good-hearted people can often say things that are painful and unhelpful. Generally the most meaningful response is something on the order of, "I'm so sorry for your loss; you're in my prayers." One family member indicated that every time someone said, "I know this must be hard," she wanted to scream out, "No you don't; you have no idea what I'm experiencing!" Also respect the family's emotional privacy. They may feel numb, or as if they are on display. Family members I interviewed indicated that they felt guilty when they didn't cry and publicly exposed when they did. Again, a simple pat on the shoulder and "You're in my prayers" can be helpful.

4. Respect the family's decisions.

If the family chooses cremation, respect the decision. If the family chooses a closed casket, respect that choice too. If the family chooses a small private funeral, respect that preference. The church is free to hold a memorial service for its own healing later. In the case of large-scale loss, such as the Oklahoma City bombing, many public services may be held. Often these are helpful to the thousands of people who cannot attend a funeral service. Such events may, however, serve a number of additional purposes, such as the gathering of community leaders, providing an "official" mourning of the tragedy. We should realize that these services are not for the family but are clearly for others.

Visitation with the family should be planned to meet family members' needs first and the community's needs second. In both the Northminster Presbyterian and First Baptist settings the visitation prior to the memorial service was scheduled at the family's request. Visitation hours in such tragedies should be coordinated by the funeral home and should respect family members' energy levels. In such situations it is not uncommon for the lines of callers to be quite long. Most funeral homes are adept at managing such scenarios and should be the primary leaders in planning the visitation, even when it is held in the church.

5. Remember that after the initial crisis is over, family members continue to struggle with their shattered lives.

For the congregation and community, the trauma is about a tragedy that happened. For family members it is about the loss of a father, a mother, a child. The degree of grief and stress is far more intense. For surviving spouses of clergy, the grief may involve not only the loss of a loved one but also the loss of an income, a place to live, and a role in the church.

We should not necessarily expect families to view the church as the place where they can heal. Each time they step back into the building may remind them that things can never again be the same. Although that may be an important step in the healing process for some, it cannot be assumed to be such for all. For some individuals, finding another church where their broken hearts can be mended is the most helpful decision. Helping a congregation eager to assist in the healing process to understand this decision is no easy task. Members may feel rejected that the family isn't at worship, especially "after all we've done for them."

The interim leadership of the congregation needs to address this issue openly and lovingly. Although *we* may want the bereaved family here as part of our healing, we have to respect that for the family, healing may best occur elsewhere. Decisions about manse/parsonage/rectory occupancy and related issues should be handled in a caring way, but in the end, it is easier for a family to know they have use of the clergy residence for six months than to have an ambiguous, open-ended agreement. Families need to know their circumstances to begin reordering life.

Follow-up care from close friends and associates is important. The burden of asking for care should not be put on those needing it. The often-used expression "Call if you need anything" is rarely helpful in the life of a hurting family member. Instead, close friends should take the initiative to check in periodically with the family. This contact can be made in unintrusive ways that respect the privacy of the family yet leave the door open for further contact.

The judicatory can be helpful in assisting leaders of the congregation to develop an appropriate means for addressing such issues. The judicatory can also provide financial information for the family on denominational insurance policies or emergency financial support.

In large-scale trauma, such as the Oklahoma City bombing, it may be more difficult to reach families in need. Many of the pastors I interviewed volunteered as chaplains but had in their congregations few or no fatalities or survivors of those killed in the blast. The community of faith provided support for families in ways described earlier in this book.

Another significant event organized out of the concern for survivors or families of victims was initiated by Westminster Presbyterian Church in Oklahoma City. Dr. Michael Anderson, senior minister, believed that the Oklahoma Arts Institute could help survivors and families by offering art as a tool for healing. Through the initiation of Dr. Anderson and the financial support of Westminster Church and the National Endowment for the Arts, 140 adults, teens, and children gathered on October 19, 1995, exactly six months after the bombing, at Quartz Mountain in Lone Wolf, Oklahoma, to participate in a four-day institute in the arts. The "Celebration of the Spirit" workshop allowed participants to reflect on their experience, share their grief, and identify hope through personal essays, poetry, Cherokee basket-weaving, memory-box sculpture, mask-making, and mixed media. Additional activities included gospel singing, dance, and painting. Volunteering to teach these classes were renowned artists from across the country.[1] This is a good example of the religious community's partnership with others for the sake of ongoing care of survivors, victims, and their families.

Caring for the Staff

In most trauma settings the staff must continue to work through the period immediately following the trauma. Administrative assistants, music leaders, and pastors are busy planning for congregational care and worship services. In the long haul, however, what happens immediately to support the staff members sets the stage for their healing. Key steps in caring for staff include the following:

1. Maintain an orderly management of work created by the trauma.

Many individuals find that having a task to do helps them to cope during the "numbing" stage following trauma. It is natural for church office workers and pastoral/programmatic staff to want to pitch in and "just do my job." Obviously there are many necessary details and tasks which the office staff is best equipped to handle. Someone in the trauma setting should be named "coordinator of office staff" during this time. If there is an office manager or business manager, this person would likely play that role. If not, I would recommend a key congregational leader filling this need for at least the first week to allow pastoral staff to give attention to the unfolding needs of the situation.

This person, appointed by either the pastoral team or the congregational governing board, should be considered part of the pastoral staff during this time to allow for communication about what is happening between the decision-makers and the office team. At Northminster the chair of the personnel committee became that person and worked extensively beyond the first weeks to help bring stability and nurture to the staff. Making a list of all the things to be done and giving clear assignments to the office staff provide focus in the midst of a chaotic environment. Avoid extending working hours unless it is absolutely essential to accomplish an important time-bound task. Staff members need the rest of the evening to sort through the events of the day and to deal with their own feelings.

2. Immediately address any safety factors involved.

If the trauma is crime-related, it is imperative that security be stepped up for all involved. Changing locks on doors, installing alarm systems, hiring security guards—whatever it takes to make people feel safe in the building should be done. Some churches have installed "panic buttons" at each administrative assistant's desk that can silently alert police to an emergency. Providing escort service to cars after dark could help people feel safe. Later, a safety assessment might be done by the local sheriff or police department to advise the church on after-dark lighting and landscaping that may need to be modified for safety. Surprising numbers of churches have large bushes or shrubs near doors or walkways that make perfect hiding places for those having no good intent. I strongly recommend holding a meeting with safety officials that includes the entire staff.

3. Protect staff from media intrusion.

Americans demand the inside scoop, and most media professionals feel compelled to respond. For that reason, reporters and others often seek out people who they think can give them the most information about the situation or the individuals involved. That usually includes the staff who have worked closely with the victims at the church that has been trauma- tized. During the immediate fallout from the trauma, it is important that staff be briefed on ways of handling the media, should they be ap- proached. Make every attempt to keep the media out of the church offices so that pressing work can get done. Having a microphone pushed in one's face or receiving unsolicited phone calls at home from an in- trusive reporter are not pleasant experiences for anyone. Staff members need to be coached on how to deal with such situations should they oc- cur. Not every TV or print reporter is offensive, but let's face it—they are aggressive. We've made it their job.

4. Provide accurate and timely information about the situation, remembering to update people in administrative roles who may not be privy to the unfolding drama.

Things happen quickly in the hours after a trauma. As the situation un- folds, it is easy to exclude the workers who are holding up the fort. The person appointed as office coordinator needs to remember to give up- dates regularly. One way to ensure follow-through is to spend the first and last 20 minutes of each day with all staff together to give the up- date, review the next day's needs, and touch base with how staff are coping. Remember, the information that can be given, should be given. This practice builds a team and helps everyone feel included. Be certain not to exclude the custodial staff from these meetings. They often are the last to know anything, yet their presence and work in the building are critical for all the meetings and gatherings ahead.

5. Provide immediate care in a group setting with a mental-health professional to debrief feelings of sorrow, fear, and the like.

A mental-health worker should be available as soon as possible for all staff people. At Northminster the two crisis workers from St. Vincent Hospital introduced themselves to the staff the morning of the crime and remained in the building all day. The day after the murders a morning meeting was held to begin responding to information and dealing with feelings. The meeting was brief but important and provided, again, a support base from the outside for those needing it. Most individuals will not take advantage of on-the-spot counseling but feel better when they have a name, face, and presence available to them.

6. Provide a critical stress debriefing for individuals at the trauma scene.

A debriefing is essential for individuals who were present at a trauma scene. It can be modified for use with individuals key to the trauma such as the staff. When Kay Schrader of St. Vincent Stress Centers met with the entire staff to conduct this debriefing, she began with those on the scene and moved to each successive member of the staff. She started by asking, "Where were you when you heard the news? What were your feelings at hearing it?" and moved on through a series of related questions. For those of us at the Mathias murder scene the process involved identifying smells, sounds, and emotional feelings in addition to what we saw. A skilled facilitator, Kay helped us anchor the memories so that we could recognize the "triggers" that touch off a return to the emotions of the event long after we think closure has occurred.

At the Oklahoma City bombing site, attempts were made to "debrief" volunteer chaplains on a regular basis, but no formal critical-incident debriefing was scheduled for several months. Obviously the chaotic nature of the event did not lend itself to any one group being responsible for such a program, and this state of affairs resulted in chaplains looking to family members and close friends to reflect on what they'd experienced. When the opportunity to "debrief" presented itself, many pastors felt it came too late. I asked one pastor who served as chaplain who debriefed him. His response was "No one. I was left to figure things out on my own."

Joe Williams, director of chaplaincy for the Department of Cooperative Mission of the Baptist General Convention of Oklahoma and chaplain for the FBI's Oklahoma Division, recognized this need. Joe organized and led a series of critical-incident workshops that began shortly after the bombing. Members of the police and fire departments, FBI, Secret Service, highway patrol, survivors, and families of victims attended these three-day events. Very few pastors availed themselves of this opportunity—a sign that clergy often feel they are capable of handling stress on their own. Encouragement needs to be given to all volunteers—lay and clergy—who provide on-site trauma care to participate in similar debriefings. Planning for such post-trauma sessions should be part of the preparation strategy for any community and should include volunteers from the religious community as its client focus.

7. Design a program of ongoing support for the staff team during months ahead.

This program should include several "temperature-taking" sessions with a mental health professional. Having one person to reflect with the team as a whole on the issues, awareness, and needs as the first year progresses is helpful. This program also prepares the staff for upcoming events, such as significant holidays that uncork emotions or the approaching anniversary of the trauma. Members of the church's personnel committee can also help by checking in at staff meetings from time to time to express interest and concern about how the staff is managing the post-trauma stress. Recognizing the staff's help during the trauma is also important. Northminster held a staff-recognition luncheon and gave personalized plaques to each as a thank-you for heroic performance of duties.

8. Provide, when possible, resources for individual counseling.

When staff members have been present at the trauma scene or its aftermath, it is important that they be offered professional help in their own recovery period. A staff is one of the church's highest investments, regardless of church size. These are the people who provide pastoral and programmatic services and know what makes the daily business of the church continue. It is the right thing for us to give employees the best psychological help possible, but it is also a shrewd way of protecting our investment. Losing a staff member because of personal stress or trauma fallout means countless hours and dollars in retraining. God has given you these good people with whom to work: Take care of them!

If it is financially feasible, the church should provide money for individual counseling for any staff person requesting it. Many denominational policies make counseling available for clergy but not for office workers. If your church is unable to provide this support for everyone, turn to your judicatory. Sometimes helpful neighboring congregations may be willing to contribute to a counseling fund. Certain individuals within most churches have the means to make special gifts as well. Do not be stymied by the limits of your budget. The support should be available for use at any time during the first year following the trauma. This policy ensures that a person experiencing delayed stress can use the fund at the time when it is most needed. Northminster made this support available to any staff member for a period of one year, even if the staffer left the employment of the church during that time.

Names of a variety of counselors should be provided on a list shared with everyone. Confidentiality can be protected by asking the service provider to contact the church treasurer for a procedure for submitting bills and to determine the dollar limit. This policy should be explained in a letter to each staff member so the counselor knows whom to contact. It is important to build an environment in which counseling is seen as a step forward, not as a step for someone who isn't coping well. If a member of the staff is able to talk openly about how helpful counseling is for him or her in coping with the aftermath, it encourages others and says, "It's OK to get help." I have talked frequently with members of the presbytery I serve about my own decision to return to a therapist following the Northminster murders. I found that having a relationship to serve as a sounding board and to check my own healing process was immensely helpful.

9. Be respectful, but don't contribute to building a shrine.

One of the most difficult issues is tactfully dealing with the possessions or "space" of someone who has died. If the trauma involves someone who has an office or desk at the church, decisions about the immediate or future use of the space should be made soon. Naturally, the family has the prerogative of going through personal possessions, and no one should disturb these things prematurely. However, decisions about computer files and other work-related materials will have to be made by someone equipped to assess their importance. Selecting a member of the staff who has good counseling and listening skills to talk with the family is a helpful way to begin this task. Don't handicap your staff because the stewardship records are on the pastor's computer and no one feels comfortable going into the files. The same is true for the office space itself. Once the family has removed personal items, open the office so that the space can be reclaimed for use.

This issue came to my attention when a candidate for the interim pastor position at Northminster told me that he was shown the building but not the pastor's office. At an unconscious level, Fred's office had become sacred space. No one was deliberately protecting or avoiding it, but the door had been kept closed since the family left. People need to see the office empty of possessions with which they identified the occupant. Of course it's hard to look in and see that the familiar items are gone. This, too, is part of acknowledging the reality of what has happened and helps the church move toward closure.

Finally, remember to expand your normal understanding of "staff." Paid musicians, seminary interns, child-care workers employed by the church—all of these should be included in your strategy for providing support.

Tasks and Care of the Official Church Decision-Makers

Normally a key group within the congregation is authorized to make decisions for the church. This important "board" may be called the session, the vestry, the council, or some other title. When the trauma to the congregation involves the pastor, this group will likely be expected to manage its grief and shock while making decisions that lay the groundwork for the next crucial days in the life of the congregation. When the trauma does not involve the pastor, these decisions are generally made in partnership with the pastor. Denominational polity also shapes how decisions are made and what outside resources might be available to these leaders. It is hard for many of us to imagine the burden that individuals in key leadership roles must feel following such events. Their aching hearts may be even heavier because of a personal relationship that deepened through working closely with the pastor in the central work of the church. They or those whom they know and love may have been personally affected by the tragedy. Yet God seems to give the strength and the wisdom to help these leaders rise to the occasion and provide direction for God's people. We will now examine some of the issues that need to be covered in the first days and months following the trauma.

1. Provide updates on the investigation.

Key leaders need accurate, immediate information. Developing a plan to communicate regularly with the board is essential. Leaders ought not have to learn from the daily paper the information they should have received through other channels. Further, the decision as to how the congregation will hear about the investigation in criminal proceedings is important. At Northminster the session, at the recommendation of the care team (described later in this chapter), decided to give an update each Sunday after worship. Mark Moore, the elder serving as spokesperson for the church, provided the update. At the encouragement of the stress counselors working with the church, this time was reserved even when there was nothing to report. Sometimes all that could be said was, "The detectives are interviewing several key leads and hope to have more information for us shortly." The session reviewed this practice after three months and went to monthly meetings when it became clear that an arrest was not imminent. The church also installed an information phone line with a recorded "update" and the capacity for callers to leave a message. Only one person had access to the informational line and relayed all relevant information to the sheriff's department. This safeguard was important to protect the confidentiality of the caller and to manage rumors or crank calls.

2. Obtain pastoral leadership.

When the church has lost its pastor in the trauma, anxiety naturally focuses on the selection of new clergy leadership. I cannot emphasize enough the importance of this decision for the future healing of the congregation. At Northminster, a beloved associate pastor of 30 years provided the significant and immediate care that many members required for the six months it took to locate the "right" interim pastor. Although he did an excellent job, his accomplishment was not without great personal cost. The stress and demands on him prevented his own natural grieving from proceeding at a normal pace, as he sacrificed for those whom he was called to serve. Associate Pastor Donna Wells agreed to extend her service beyond her original resignation date to the end of January to care for those closest to her ministry.

The presbytery, through its committee on ministry that counsels churches on pastoral relationships, appointed a pastor to lead session meetings, thus freeing the two associate pastors to focus on the pastoral care of the congregation during the search for an interim. The pastoral load was heavy. For other churches, administration could be brokered out in a different way. Fortunately, the temporary moderator, a minister who served as director of a family-life center at a nearby Presbyterian church, was known to the congregation. His counseling background allowed him to approach difficult subjects and decisions in gentle ways.

Choosing or appointing the right pastor after the trauma is one of the most important decisions that can be made. In polities where the pastor is appointed by a bishop, it would be wise for this pastor to be chosen for a shorter, transitional ministry rather than a longer period of leadership. Naturally pastoral-care skills are important, but so is the ability to discern the unfolding nature of grief and to be able to help a congregation in "moving on" at a pace that is often difficult to predict. For several reasons, I would discourage using a pastor who already serves the congregation in some capacity to fill this role. First, the pastor is dealing with his or her own issues and grief, which should not be postponed or denied for the sake of serving the church. Secondly, no one can replace the lost pastor—not even someone who already has a special place in the congregation's heart. Third, the associate or other pastor was not called to serve as head of staff, and a crisis is probably not the best time to learn those skills. The congregation may place pressure on the appointive or advisory system, saying that the associate "knows us" or "we owe it to him" (or her), but these reactions reflect the anxiety of the unknown placed on an already unstable congregation. It is not, in my opinion, wise to yield to this pressure.

In denominations where congregations conduct a search for new pastors, they often use a professional interim pastor to assist them through the transition. Many individuals are especially trained to assist congregations amid the change, grief, and critical decision-making that come between installed pastorates. In highly traumatized situations, the search committee for interim leadership will want to add skills in pastoral care or crisis management to the list of desired attributes. Many denominations have professional associations for clergy serving as interim pastors. The ecumenical association is the Interim Ministry Network. Membership in these associations generally indicates that pastors are serious about transitional leadership.

At First Baptist in Shelbyville, the interim pastor who came shortly after Martin Travelstead's death was a retired pastor known to the congregation with proven skills in pastoral care. At Northminster, the presbytery worked with the personnel committee of the church to find a pastor who was serving as head of staff in a larger-membership congregation, who had experience in leading a multiple staff, who was an excellent preacher, and who had a good track record in pastoral care. Since the immediate needs of the congregation were not the traditional "interim tasks," it was agreed that the Rev. Ronald Smith would wait to take interim pastor training until his second year of leadership with the church. The importance of this delay to the care of the decision-makers is that they, too, needed a sense of stability before making long-term decisions.

The typical one-year interim period is not applicable to this setting. The interim period between the loss of the pastor through trauma and the arrival of a more permanent pastor will vary according to the situation. At Northminster, because of the shattering nature of the trauma, the uncertainty of a potential arrest and trial of the perpetrators, and the fact that Frederick Mathias had served for 13 years and had been approaching retirement, it was recommended to the session that the interim period be considered at least three years. It is imperative, however, that this time frame not be rushed even when the congregation thinks that moving with dispatch is in its best interest. Choosing another pastor while in the midst of anger, pain, and grief is like selecting one's next spouse the week after the deceased spouse's funeral. Such choices are rarely healthy ones.

3. Care for the congregation.

In addition to the plan for interim leadership, the board must make immediate decisions about follow-up care for the congregation. The strategy for Northminster was the formation of a "care team" (see Appendix A) appointed by the session. In smaller-membership congregations many of these functions might be managed by the interim pastor with assistance from community mental health workers.

4. Tend to lay leaders who are severely traumatized.

Someone needs to track the stress level of lay leaders who may have been severely affected by the trauma. Because they often have tasks similar to those of staff members, they may appear to be coping with the tragedy better than they really are. The more a member has direct contact with the pastor, the more affected he can be by the pastor's death. We should remember that events in a particular leader's life may have rendered her even more vulnerable to the current trauma. Outside helpers can be sensitive to this reality, and, if steered to those leaders in need of special care, can be certain they are ministered to. The care team mentioned above focused on the importance of team building, effective communication, good conflict management, and stress management in its work with the session. One discussion was spent on the expectations that the church had of its lay leaders and how crisis or disequilibrium affects the fulfillment of that role. The leaders were particularly sensitive to the elders serving on session who had special needs.

Outside helpers from the judicatory should be certain to remember the importance of "checking in" with the decision-makers on a three-month, six-month, and one-year schedule following the trauma. Sometimes these visits are for the purpose of offering concrete help, at other times just for the moral and spiritual support of those serving in lay leadership roles. Visiting with the board is also a way of "taking the temperature" of the congregation.

5. Make other business-related decisions.

Depending on the dynamics of the trauma, economic decisions may need to be made. Determining the use of undesignated memorial gifts, estimating the costs of funeral expenses or other special service costs, authorizing financial support for counseling of staff—all these may be under the responsibilities of the board.

Caring for the Congregation—The Importance of a Plan

As I discuss the importance of caring for the congregation in an organized, careful way, I will remind the reader that these ideas need to be adjusted in light of issues such as congregational size, available leadership, and nature of the trauma. I believe, however, that the strategy used by Northminster has helpful ideas and insights for every situation, even if the scope of the plan is not appropriate for each.

One of the first recommendations I made to the session at Northminster in late December 1996 was the formation of a "care team." These individuals needed to be members of the congregation from the helping professions who were willing to work with the session in planning the wide scope of congregational care that would be required in a church of almost 2,000 members. The session approved the recommendation and appointed an eight-member team chaired by Marianne Hedges, an elder serving on the session. Marianne was a social worker at the Marion County Children's Guardian Home. Other members of the team included a probation supervisor from the Marion County Juvenile Probation Court; a social worker from a local hospital; a volunteer with a hospice program; a retired couple who had previously expressed an interest in developing a structure for helping relationships among Northminster members; Kimberly Koczan, the member of the staff carrying the portfolio of group life coordinator; and the Rev. Carol McDonald, who had chosen Northminster as her worship community when joining the staff of the Synod of Lincoln Trails as educator and vocational specialist. They defined their role as follows:

I. Goals
- To provide resources and support for the congregation in managing grief, anger, and other emotions that naturally arise in situations of violent loss.
- In consultation with staff, to anticipate theological issues or matters of faith that may need to be addressed.
- To facilitate and monitor the healing process.

II. Time Frame
- Care team to be in place as long as needed.
- Anticipated healing process of at least 12 months.
- Division of the year's work in six-week segments for assessment.

III. Membership
- Ad hoc team of Northminster members.
- Team to report directly to the session.

IV. Responsibilities
- Planning healing-related activities.
- Coordinating activities through normal church systems such as business administrator (scheduling of rooms, etc.), session, and staff.
- Maintaining awareness of the changing care needs of the congregation and staff.
- Providing a balance of therapeutic and theological activities.
- Communicating times, places, and types of activities offered to the congregation.
- Choosing outside grief counselors as needed.
- Planning for information sessions as the investigation unfolds.
- Planning worship occasions.
- Facilitating the return to normal and familiar routines.

The complete outline of the care team's goals and objectives can be found in appendix A. The following is a summary of some of its activities and learning through the difficult year of its work.

The Importance of Remembering

It was noted early on by the care team that Northminster members had not been able to say good-bye to the pastor and his wife as they would have hoped in a retirement celebration. Even though there had been prayer services, a chance to visit with the Mathias children, and a memorial service, it didn't seem enough. People were still in shock during these opportunities. The care team therefore sought to provide a variety of occasions for remembering and coming to closure. Hundreds of sympathy cards, letters, and gifts came from across the country. These were collected and placed in memorial books in the church library. One of the most touching was a gift that arrived the week after the murders— paper origami doves made by members of a small Presbyterian church in Montana. These were used on the communion table that Sunday in worship and then moved to the library for viewing.

Northminster members and friends were encouraged to write their own memories and to contribute photographs of the Mathias family to these books. The first six months following the murders saw a "Fred and Cleta—We Remember" bulletin board in the narthex. Items from church members were removed periodically to make room for additional items to be displayed. When removed, items went to the memory book. This display proved quite effective and was often a topic of conversation among members as the display changed. At the end of the six months it was taken down as another gentle, symbolic way of indicating that the grief period had shifted to another stage.

The Importance of Talking

Each Thursday evening for the first six months "A Time to Talk" was held from 5:30 to 6:30 P.M. in the church parlor. This opportunity for members to get together to share feelings and gain support was informally led. During the first six months after the trauma, two six-week series of bereavement support groups were sponsored jointly by the St. Vincent Stress Centers and the care team for members of the congregation. The care team continued to be fascinated by the fact that these groups drew very few people. It was only in conducting research for this book that I discovered, reading Lula Redmond's *Surviving: When Someone You Love Was Murdered,* that grief groups are often ineffective until at least six months after the loss. Most people are still in a state of trauma, or the delayed stress has not yet hit. Offering these groups too soon and discontinuing them at about the time they may have begun to work is, I believe, the only mistake made in the care strategy of the congregation. I share it only as information for the reader, not in criticism of the care team, which charted new ground in pastoral care.

The Importance of Education

Many educational opportunities were given to the church family over the following year. "Safety for All Seasons" was a seminar on personal safety led by the coordinator of the Indianapolis Police Department Crime Watch. A certified massage therapist and counselor led several sessions on the physical effects of emotional trauma on the body. Margaret Anne Huffman, author of *"Through the Valley..." Prayers for Violent Times* led an adult church-school class. Carol McDonald, a member of the care team, led sessions for parents of young children and others in the congregation on using children's books to deal with grief and anxiety. Special books were purchased for the library and reviewed in the newsletter. Each edition of *News and Views*, the church newsletter, featured a page from the care team full of ideas, resources, and opportunities to assist the church in the grief process. These are only a few examples from the educational strategy.

Responding to Particular Communities

Homebound Members

One of the most overlooked parts of the congregation during trauma is the homebound membership. These members are unable to attend church to hear any of the updates or to participate in any of the services or programs for healing. Jody and Bob Baumgardt, members of the care team, agreed to work with the deacons at Northminster in making certain that these elderly, ill, or disabled members were not slighted in the care process. The deacons had distributed memorial flowers and Christmas poinsettias to the homebound and to members in nursing homes immediately after the murders and memorial services. They were delighted to be useful in helping these members and attended a training session full of questions and ideas. They were given a sheet with suggestions on how to conduct an informational visit. It included accurate information which they could communicate to the confined member.

The suggested outline began with expressing the church's concern that the member be fully informed about the church's present status. Visitors were urged to begin by asking, "Do you feel that you know enough about the details of the case?" This opening was intended to protect older members who found the details upsetting and didn't want to know them. Next, visitors were to ask, "Would you like to share with me what you do know?" to look for errors or holes in their information. Then callers were to ask if members had questions, how they were feeling, and if there was anything further the church could do. A fact sheet given to each visitor included information about the investigation, the reward offered, and the status of the church and its pastors.

The homebound members were treated with respect as full members of the community of faith, and so the visitor let them know there were several things they could do—pray for the church and its staff, pray for the Mathias family, pray for all who were working to solve the crime and for the perpetrators. If members wanted the information, they were told that memorial gifts could be sent to the church office. The visitors were given copies of three inspirational readings and poems either to read during the visit or to leave with the member. The Sunday updates on the investigation were printed so that visitors could take the most recent one on each call made during the next six months. It was also explained to homebound members that they could expect to see more deacons and fewer pastors during the immediate transition since the pastors were desperately needed to manage the church until an interim pastor was called.

Care for Young Children

The number-one concern for parents is the safety of their child. When the trauma has been a violent incident, providing safety and communicating with parents is of utmost importance. Secondly, parents in church settings often are uncertain how to handle information. What should the young child be told? Third, what signs should alert them that the child may be having problems that stem from the trauma?

The church should anticipate such concerns and be prepared to address them. Parents themselves may experience conflicting emotions, and this anxiety will also influence how they respond to their children and the church. It is imperative for us to communicate to parents the importance of their role in assuring their children that their concerns are normal and valid. Younger children, especially, are emotionally vulnerable and look to parents to protect them. In the appendixes are several helpful resources for use with children and parents, including a list of children's books dealing with trauma and death. Particularly helpful is "Children, Youth and Grief," which identifies the way children and youth of approximate ages approach death and grief.[2]

Northminster began its assistance to children by providing a leaflet for parents at the very first prayer gathering the night after the murders. This resource suggested ways the parent might talk to the child and identified signs of stress that might alert the parent to unmanaged fear or confusion. The care team also provided three adult church-school sessions for parents of children, led by a mental health professional. Children's books were listed in the newsletter and available in the library. Sunday-school teachers attended a similar session that focused on handling children's questions and working closely with parents.

Caring for Youth

Teen-age youth are easily overwhelmed by the emotions that accompany their developmental process. The teen who experiences a significant loss is even more likely to be overwhelmed. Teens are even less likely to reach out for help than grieving adults. It is important that the church be a place where teenagers are encouraged to grieve. When whole groups of teens are in grief, tears cannot be held back. It is important that youth leaders give permission for them to express grief in a supervised setting. The role of mental-health professionals in working with youth groups cannot be overemphasized. Since many church traditions place confirmation during the teen years, issues of faith and theology may be very much on the minds of many young people. Do not shy away from these issues of belief. If the youth leaders do not feel skilled in this area, look for a local clergyperson or other theologically trained individual who can work with the group. Do not underestimate the teenagers' ability to integrate their budding theology with what has happened. Trauma can be a time of growing faith as well as a time of testing faith. Again, the appendixes include resources for understanding and working with this age group.

The strategy for working with the youth at Northminster was complicated by the fact that a young person was a primary suspect in the investigation. Rumors quickly began to fly which could be neither validated nor dismissed because of the confidentiality of the investigation. Five young men in the youth group had moved a rug at the Mathias home the day before the murders, and the sheriff's department questioned each of them extensively in the early stages of the investigation. Security was increased when the youth groups were meeting. One of the young men in question quickly dropped out of the group's activities, a development that further heightened the rumors as time went on.

Nevertheless, work needed to be done to assist the teens in their own grief work. A special forum was held for the youth group, where questions of faith and theology were raised. Lots of "one-on-ones" took place between the youth minister and individual youth. In midsummer an exposé article was published in the *Indianapolis Star,* pointing again to this former youth-group member as the prime suspect. Another round of conversations and group work was needed to deal with reactions to the article. After the arrest of the youth more than a year later, the youth group had several sessions with a mental-health worker and their youth leaders to assist them in dealing with their feelings of anger and betrayal that one of their own may have committed the horrible crime. Many youth participated in the adult activities offered within the church as well as those directed specifically at youth.

Measuring Health and Healing

When the Northminster Care Team reflected on its work a year later, it identified the following signs of healing in the church:

1.   More realism and comfort were expressed with the way things stood; less effort was expended in trying to make things the way they used to be.

2.   New and healthy relationships had been established, especially with the interim pastor.

3.   People were becoming more open to change instead of clinging to the comfort of the past.

4.   The congregation was accepting the responsibility as a church family to work together to create meaning and purpose in the new reality that was emerging.

5.   An ability was shown to acknowledge the new or unused gifts and

skills within the church discovered during the grief and healing process.

6. Members and leaders adjusted to role changes.

7. The church began to organize and plan for the future.

Caring for the Extended Church

Judicatory leaders should be aware that the ripples of pain, fear, and depression extend far beyond the particular congregation affected. Pastors and their families have the same anxieties that any population group suffers in highly traumatized settings. When violence has occurred, it is imperative that these individuals be given care and comfort, as well as those directly affected by the tragedy. Often they are forgotten in the rush of immediate need following the event. A judicatory staff member or leader can do several things to provide support for those marginally affected.

1. Provide information

A pastoral letter providing accurate information to date should be sent to all pastors and key judicatory leaders. Such a letter not only informs the body of the currently known details of the situation but also provides a sense of comfort that the judicatory is involved and is providing support. It should include not only the specifics of the occurrence but as much about the care of the congregation and affected individuals as can be told at the time. Names and addresses of survivors can be listed for the benefit of those who wish to write personal notes. Generally this letter should not be the primary way of informing people about the memorial service. A telephone tree from the judicatory office can communicate such information in a much more timely fashion. I suggest a follow-up letter with an update to the leaders and pastors of the judicatory about two weeks following the incident.

2. Dispel rumors

In some situations the rumors are the most damaging part of a tragedy. On the morning of the Mathias murders, people waiting in the small chapel observed the seals of the Apostles displayed on the walls. It was noted that St. Matthew's seal featured crossed battle axes—also the instruments of Fred Mathias' death. Shortly thereafter it was rumored that a serial killer was targeting all clergy with biblical names. Although it may sound absurd to the reader, it was very real to those horrified by the unexplainable events of December 15.

This rumor was further exacerbated by the grapevine analysis of a popular television show that aired two weeks before the murders, featuring an account of a minister axed by an emotionally disturbed individual. Thus, a second set of rumors began to circulate through our judicatory.

The final straw for me was the rumor that Fred and Cleta Mathias had been murdered because of a position they took on a political issue facing our denomination. The tale was offensive to me partly because the pastor had not been outspoken on this issue and also because it maligned our denomination, suggesting that emotions ran high enough to lead to murder. Nevertheless, it is the judicatory head's job to dispel such speculations quickly and carefully with as much grace and firmness as he or she can muster.

3. Astutely observe those who may need extra care

The personal friendships that may exist between those directly affected by the trauma and others in the judicatory should not be neglected. It is easy to forget that deep friendships outside the church family are also traumatized. Who needs extra care in the judicatory as a result of this trauma, and how will that care be given? This is an important question to consider in planning the judicatory strategy.

4. Public prayer and regular reporting

Remembering to pray about the tragedy and those affected is important for the healing of the judicatory. For at least the first six months, the names of those involved and the congregation should be listed in judicatory communications and included in public prayer. If there are ways in which neighboring congregations or pastors can help the affected church, they should be shared through such means.

The magnitude of human need that results from trauma can easily overwhelm us. "When in doubt, do nothing" is the worst possible posture. The careful planning of a care strategy uniquely tailored to all the groups and individuals affected by the trauma results in the faithful fulfillment of God's command to love one another. Not all of the strategies suggested in this chapter will be helpful in every situation. I hope they will provide a guide to the development of a plan to fit the needs of each unfolding situation.

CHAPTER 6

Worship as a Tool for Healing

Praise without lament is not honest; accept our grief as evidence of our trust in you.

—Margaret Anne Huffman,
"Through the Valley..." Prayers for Violent Times, p. 127

The power of the Holy Spirit, the resources of the therapeutic community, the support and nurture of others, the gift of time—all are important to the healing process. Nothing, however, is more important to the person of faith than the powerful resource of worship. Worship does many things. It provides one with "safe" space for grieving, remembering, and, later, for renewal. Through the beauty of the liturgy or familiarity with the order of worship, participants are invited into a state of dependency on God where the pain of life can be released. The music triggers much-needed tears or, later in the healing process, lifts the broken hearts in hope. It is where those gathered hear the Word of God *for each of them.* It is where others hold up the weak and place them in God's hands. It is one of the most precious gifts and greatest resources of the Christian faith. Never should worship be more carefully planned than in the months following a traumatic event. For some, it may be a matter of life or death.

We Cannot Use What's Not Already There

In thinking about the role of worship in the healing of a congregation, it is important to note that the time of grief, anger, and disillusionment is not the time to strengthen a worship program. Carol McDonald, associate executive of the Synod of Lincoln Trails and a Presbyterian minister who worships at Northminster, states, "Northminster's trauma has convinced me, more firmly than ever, that a strong worship life must be in place and must continue for a congregation to be able to survive and learn from such a shocking horror."[1] Ministerial staffs who work closely with musicians and other worship leaders in planning weekly experiences to reflect a common theme have the strongest base from which to plan worship in times of trauma. Even in nonliturgical traditions the way Scripture, music, prayers, and the message complement one another can make a large difference in the healing process for parishioners. In our public ministries to those who grieve we must draw upon the rituals and words that help us to weld the community together and to make sense of the tragedy of life. If we have a holistic approach to planning worship in nonstressful times, we can depend upon those skills for the critical task of worship during the stressful ones.

Funerals and Memorial Services

When the trauma has been marked by death, the church will gather for a funeral or memorial service. The distinction between the two terms is influenced by custom, the faith tradition, and the culture of the community. Often a funeral precedes a burial and is conducted with the remains present. It may be called a memorial service if it is held following a committal or when the remains are not present. Whatever term is used, it is an opportunity for the community of believers to gather for a service of worship that recognizes the reality of death, offers comfort to those who mourn, and reminds us of Christ's victory over death. The nature of the trauma will most certainly shape the mood and direction of the service.

Rituals help us to manage the powerful feelings triggered by loss. The funeral or memorial service is primarily a ritual of ending. The belief that it is also a beginning, as in our resurrection theology, should be present but should not overshadow the reality of death so that the fundamental identity of the service is lost.[2] Almost all denominations have plans for funerals, memorial services, and graveside services in their books of worship. Many other excellent resources are available in Christian publications. The important thing to remember in planning the service is that those who grieve need to be connected to the larger reality of God and God's love for us.

If there are surviving family members, their wishes regarding the service should be of paramount consideration. Pastors, however, should be prepared to make suggestions since trauma is unexpected and generally involves shock. Family members may not be able to participate in planning the service because of their own emotional struggle. Sensitivity to the family's emotional state is important in estimating the length of the service. If there are to be memorial moments or eulogies, be realistic about the number of speakers. The funeral is not a political occasion on which every person who has known the deceased must have an opportunity to reflect. Putting families through lengthy services at a time when they are already exhausted is not helpful. I recognize, however, that funerals are culturally based experiences and that they will vary in length and other dimensions in accord with a church's liturgical practice and its regional, racial, or ethnic tradition. If the person's role or life has had a high profile and it is appropriate for many individuals to be included, a memorial service later may be a better choice for the public remembering.

The location for the funeral or memorial service is also a critical decision. Holding the service in the church is meaningful to the congregation but may not accommodate the anticipated attendance of the community. Moving the service to another church or to a public site such as a high school auditorium or gymnasium allows for more participation but does not provide the "comfort" of the church where the deceased lived out his or her faith. It is a judgment call. Northminster decided to keep the service in its own sanctuary, using closed-circuit television for the overflow crowd in the fellowship hall. At First Baptist in Shelbyville, the service was moved to another church because of the fire damage and the desire to accommodate a large crowd. Mortuaries rarely have adequate space for a service following a tragedy.

Large community memorial services following tragedies are common. They are generally most meaningful to people who did not know the deceased personally, when there are multiple deaths, or when an entire community has been affected by the death. Tens of thousands of people came to the State Fair Arena in Oklahoma City for the national service of prayer on April 23, 1995. Cathy Keating, first lady of Oklahoma, organized the service, which was attended by President and Mrs. Clinton and by the Rev. Billy Graham, who brought words of comfort to a grieving nation. The service was televised nationally. These are important, public acknowledgments of what has happened. They cannot, however, replace the intimate role of the funeral or memorial service.

The Challenge of Preaching

Preaching that fosters denial is not useful. There will always be those who prefer that worship be uplifting, that it focus only on the positive and the promises of healing. We must remember, however, that the Christian faith involves both the cross and the empty tomb. Preachers have a unique opportunity to provide a balance between those two important aspects of faith and to bring them to bear on the trauma at hand.

Preaching can serve four important tasks in ministering to the bereaved: maintaining faithful contact with reality, dealing with what the Scriptures tell us about loss, acknowledging the theodicy problem, and granting permission for the often conflicted feelings that arise at these times. The frank recognition of loss, even when it is difficult to discuss, as in a suicide or murder, must be acknowledged to move past it. During the memorial service or funeral, the event that led to the death needs to be named for what it is—a tragedy. This service is not the place to explore theodicy at length, but it cannot be ignored. Most people gathered cannot yet be comforted by the intellectual exploration of God's role in dreadful events. But the question "Why?" can be voiced. Generally, the most authentic and comforting response is simply, "It is beyond our understanding."

Planning the Funeral or Memorial Service

At Marty Travelstead's funeral service, his childhood friend and fellow pastor John Parsley delivered the message. John did a masterful job of balancing the sadness of Marty's death with the success of his life. John admitted his own anger at Marty for the decision to end his life—a statement that surely allowed others to admit that they too felt anger. It is important to establish an environment where the words "suicide" and "took his life" are acceptable. Many people shy away from direct speech because it is uncomfortable for the speaker. The family, however, may find relief in the open and honest naming of what has happened. At the same time, John's message moved past that disappointment and into the ways God had used Marty for the good of the kingdom. He ended with words of comfort and appropriate hope. This pattern of acknowledgment, reflection, and promise brings support to those gathered and gives permission for the same pattern to be lived out in their hearts. Preachers know that the wisdom for such sermons comes from the leading of the Holy Spirit, for few of us alone would be able to know what to say.

The memorial service for Fred and Cleta Mathias reflected their love of the great traditions of the church. Congregational singing, special music provided by the Chancel Choir, and a rich liturgy were important components. The decision to include only one "memorial moment" for each of them was in keeping with Fred's commitment to worship as the focus of the funeral service. The two associate pastors and I led the worship service and delivered the memorials. The service lasted the traditional one hour so common to Presbyterians. Services in the other communities where the Mathiases had served were held later. Northminster sent an associate pastor to those services to represent the church.

At the meeting of the General Assembly of the Presbyterian Church (U.S.A.) in June 1997, a special concert of sacred music written and performed by renowned jazz musician Dave Brubeck was held in honor and memory of the ministry of Fred and Cleta Mathias. It was made possible through the memorial gifts of many congregations. By giving mourners several opportunities to "remember," worship became an ongoing part of the healing process for the whole denomination as well as for Northminster.

"Worship at the time of loss," say Anderson and Mitchell, "needs to recognize the human condition of sorrow and distress while at the same time the presence of God is remembered and claimed."[3] The preacher essentially gives legitimacy to the feelings that people are having. He or she reminds us that the Bible is full of the stories of God's

faithful servants in the midst of sorrow. When feelings are mixed—
anger, sadness, guilt, disappointment—it is even more important that
preaching grant permission to open oneself unashamedly to God through
faith. The carefully planned memorial or funeral service is the beginning
of that process.

The Ongoing Role of Worship

The funeral or memorial service is a ritual of ending, but it begins the
formal process of grief and healing. It may have been preceded by a
service of prayer and Scripture such as the one held at Northminster the
evening after the murders or the many spontaneous services of prayer
that were held across Oklahoma City the evening of the bombing. Worship, however, can continue to play an important part in the cycle of
recovery, which continues for the next year to 18 months. Some important occasions for worship that need special attention are the first
Sunday after the trauma, the arrival of a new pastor if the trauma has
resulted from the death or removal of the minister, the first round of
sacred holidays, and the first anniversary of the trauma. Each situation
may also include other particular occasions when a special service or
emphasis is appropriate.

The First Sunday after the Trauma

People are drawn to the church by a tragedy. Some come for the "news,"
but the majority come because of a feeling that the family of faith needs
to be together. In situations of natural disaster it is important for the
church to gather even if its building has been destroyed. Communities
of faith gather in school auditoriums, in the sanctuaries of neighboring
churches, or in the open space around the church if safety and weather
allow. It is vital for worship life to continue and for the church to demonstrate to the world that its rituals cannot be stopped by the unexpected jolts of life.

  In instances involving the death or removal of a pastor, selection of
the preacher for the day is critically important. Riley Walker, Southwest
Area minister of the American Baptist Churches of Indiana, preached

the Sunday after Marty Travelstead's death. Riley was well known to the congregation and had offered support and counsel in the earlier events of the week. He used Psalm 23 as his text. Robert Hunter, director of the Family Life Center at Second Presbyterian Church in Indianapolis, a pastoral counseling center, delivered the message at Northminster. In both of these settings associate pastors could have preached. The decision to invite someone outside the staff was wise in that it gave the pastors permission to grieve as well. Looking for the right person to meet the need of the congregation is an important consideration for the first public worship service following the traumatic event.

The First Sunday of a New Pastorate

The next major shift for congregations losing their minister is the presence of an interim or a new appointment. Although the Rev. Dr. Ronald Smith did not arrive at Northminster until six months after the murders, several parishioners told me that his first Sunday in the pulpit was the first time they had come to grips with the fact that Fred Mathias was not coming back. Using the familiar faces to lead worship can be helpful to the church initially, but sooner or later members must begin to let go of the former relationship. In "call system" denominations this transition can be accomplished through the skill of an interim pastor to lead during the time of healing. In appointment polities, the bishop would be wise to consider a shorter appointment focused on some of the same tasks of an interim period.

The decision to call the Rev. Wally Jeffs to serve as part-time interim pastor at First Baptist in Shelbyville was a good one. Wally had been the first senior pastor to work with Marty Travelstead after his graduation from seminary. Now retired, Wally Jeffs had years of ministerial experience in dealing with pain and loss. On his first Sunday in the pulpit he began a series of sermons on grace and the Great Commission understood in the midst of tragedy.

Ron Smith was recruited to serve as Northminster's interim pastor from First Presbyterian Church in Rochester, Minnesota, a congregation of 1,200 members. His first Sunday sermon has so many salient points that I have included it in its entirety in Appendix H. One of the promises Ron made that morning was to listen to the things that are in your hearts so that I can help you practice good stewardship of the pain you have experienced. . . . I understand my first and greatest responsibility as your pastor will be to help you find a voice to bear witness, a voice that will well up out of the darkness of this tragedy as a great song of faith to all those around us who need a faith to live by. . . . Together, we will unwrap the wounds of our hearts so that people all around us—wounded and hurting people—will see and know that they can come to Northminster Church with their broken hearts and needy lives and they will be welcomed here in Christ's name.[4]

Preaching through the Year

The task of preaching through the first year after a trauma involves a careful monitoring of the congregation's progress toward healing. Remembering that people will be in different places in their separate journeys toward wholeness, the preacher can find sermon preparation particularly challenging. For the first six months some element that can facilitate this movement should be intentionally included in each service. It does not always have to be part of the sermon but can be reflected in the prayers, liturgies, or music of the day. Gradually, as life seems to settle down, overt mention of the trauma may be replaced with more subtle, thematic references. Assessing this shift is an art and may best be determined in consultation with others. Pastors who work in churches with care committees and worship committees can use them as sounding boards for planning.

The way a pastor returns to the tragedy as time goes on is as important as the reference to the event. In a comment on preaching to traumatized congregations, Carol McDonald made an astute observation about the use of the lectionary, that cycle of biblical texts read in worship in many denominations. "If ever I doubted the validity of using the lectionary as the basis for worship," she said, "I am now firmly convinced that this resource can provide the strongest foundation possible for a congregation's worship life. . . . The lectionary provides a worshipping community with God's continuing word, the ongoing story of God's people."[5] The lectionary is the most consistent way of demonstrating that God does not break promises. The lectionary also lends itself to the biblical themes that reflect the church's journey through the liturgical cycle and the individual Christian's journey through life, a comforting foundation for an uncomfortable year.

Music Soothes the Broken Heart

Music is the poetry of the soul. Music can make us happy; it can relax us; it can conjure up imagination as well as memory. It can also free our tears or comfort our spirit. The selection of music is almost as important as the selection of a scriptural text when one is planning meaningful worship for a hurting congregation. The use of familiar hymns that remind us of God's love and care, that acknowledge the brokenness of human life, that reiterate the promises of life everlasting, are important parts of the pilgrimage through grief. Special attention should be given to organ or other instrumental music and anthems as well as congregational singing. If a smaller-membership congregation does not have the resources to expand its music library to include appropriate selections, it may wish to ask neighboring congregations or sister churches within its denomination to lend materials or even to provide special music on occasion. Again, we should not forget that most colleague congregations want to help in some way.

Among the special resources available to churches is a collection of songs from the Iona Community in Scotland titled *When Grief is Raw: Songs for Times of Sorrow and Bereavement.* In the introduction to this collection authors John Bell and Graham Maule state, "We believe that essentially a hymn should convey what God has to say to the people and/ or what the people need to say to God."[6] Acknowledging the immense range of emotion present in the Psalms, these fine composers have written easily sung hymns that allow the community of faith to sing honestly about their experience—including the raw pleading and complaining that we need to offer God in addition to praise and adoration. Arranged for congregational use to be sung a cappella or accompanied, they are also appropriate for a soloist or choir. The collection includes songs for times of grieving, consolation, petitioning God's help, leave-taking (funerals), and special circumstances such as the death of a child or disaster in a Third World nation. The booklet also contains several liturgies. Naturally, such a resource is used most effectively if the church's music library contains sufficient copies (or permission to photocopy has been secured from copyright holders) and musicians are familiar with the music before it is needed.

Often people say they are reluctant to come to church because the music "makes me cry." It is appropriate for the pastor or worship leader to remind the gathered community publicly that tears are God's way of releasing our pain. What better place to cry than in the presence of God and those who love God?

Prayers, Poems, and Psalms

Approximately half of the book of Psalms is made up of songs of lament or complaint. The richness of this part of our Bible for times of trauma cannot be overestimated. Using the Psalms as responsive readings, as texts for sermons, and as portions of prayers only scratches the surface of possible uses for this important collection of songs and poems. Using the Psalms in an adult church-school class exploring the movement of grief, anger, and petition is yet another way of assisting parishioners to understand and respond to their own emotional and spiritual issues.

The classic model of Israel's response to her own tragic moments includes six components, which appear either separately or together in various ways throughout the Psalms. These are the naming of God in a familiar way, "My God, God of my fathers"; lodging a complaint about the difficulty of life; uttering a specific petition to God; presenting a rationale for God's obligation to respond; occasionally requesting vengeance or retribution; and, oddly, often ending with joy and praise.[7] Walter Brueggeman, professor of Old Testament at Columbia Presbyterian Theological Seminary, calls this literature a "spirituality of protest." In the wake of the shootings of the kindergarten children at Dunblane Primary School, Scotland, in 1996, a minister was heard to say with dismay, "We've forgotten how to lament!"[8]

Poet Ann Weems has provided a beautifully written collection of contemporary psalms in *Psalms of Lament*. Ann and her husband, Don, a Presbyterian clergyman, lost their son Todd in a brutal murder on his 21st birthday. The crime is still unsolved. In reflecting on her own daily struggle of grief and loss, Ann says, "There is no salvation in self-help books; the help we need is far beyond self. Our only hope is to march

ourselves to the throne of God and in loud lament cry out the pain that
lives in our souls."[9] The 50 psalms she has written cover a wide range of
response and can be beautifully integrated into worship, devotional life,
or special services. As part of the healing journey a congregation could
consider holding a retreat or workshop guided by a leader trained in
grief counseling, at which one activity could be the writing of psalms of
lament. A church could assemble its own book of psalms or use them in
Sunday worship.

Symbols Can Be Powerful

In my interview with Margaret Ball, a Methodist pastor and skilled
counselor in Oklahoma City, she told me about driving into the city on
the morning after the bombing. It was still dark, and as she drove over
the hilltop expecting the usual view of the city, she saw on the side of
the Liberty Bank Building that the cross, normally reserved for the
Christmas season, had been lit. What better statement in the midst of
destruction?

In planning worship as a tool for healing we should remember the
potential power of visual symbol. During Lent we often see crosses
draped in purple outside church buildings. It would be hard for even the
casual passer-by to miss the message when the days after Easter show it
draped in white! The presence of origami paper doves on the communion
table at Northminster, a gift from Presbyterian women of the Conrad
(Montana) Presbyterian Church, allowed those gathered for worship to
see the love of others and the promise of God's peace. On the one-year
anniversary of the bombing, St. Luke's Methodist Church in Oklahoma
City tied a while ribbon on the chancel cross and laid an engraved rem-
nant of the Murrah Building on the communion table. These gestures all
enhanced the flow of worship and enabled a response that extended beyond words. Planning for worship after a traumatic event should use
every means possible to assist those who gather for worship to understand, accept, and move past what has happened to them.

Anniversaries

The most important anniversary remembrance for a traumatized church will be the first. At Northminster the occasion was marked by an Advent service of prayer and reflection focusing on the theme of light coming into a world of darkness. A memorial prayer was offered for Fred and Cleta Mathias, and the meditation acknowledged the importance of the date. In Oklahoma City the first anniversary was marked by many individual congregations and a community prayer service. In a number of these services the names of all those who had lost their lives were read. The number of people who attend these services may, interestingly enough, be small. It is important, however, to offer services for those who need to be there.

After the first anniversary it may be best not to hold a special service but rather to incorporate the acknowledgment within a regular worship occasion. Life does go on, and part of releasing the traumatic past to God's care is letting go of how trauma *defines* the congregation. Remembering is always important, but the way we remember and the intensity of focus on the remembrance should alter as time goes on. This shift is particularly difficult in settings where the trauma was crime-related and where no arrests have been made. Still, the church of Jesus Christ cannot be limited or defined by one event in its history, no matter how shattering it may have been. Anniversary times in these situations remind the congregation that there has not been closure and often bring back the feelings of sadness and loss. Special care should be taken to reinforce the healing that has occurred.

Other Services

There may be times unique to the trauma when additional services for prayer or worship are helpful. The care team at Northminster had carefully planned a prayer service in the event of an arrest. Such a service was held on the evening of January 27, 1998, when two arrests were made. The purpose of the gathering was threefold: to allow the congregation to be together as soon as possible after the arrests were announced; to pray for the surviving Mathias family, for the alleged perpetrators of the crimes and their families, and for strength in the congregation to face the next step; and to be a public witness to the community that the church, while desiring justice, did not desire vengeance.

The prayer of invocation said this well: "God of justice and compassion, you have been faithful to us in all things. You have been with us and with the Mathias family during these months of waiting. We continue to put our trust in you, praying that you will weave out of these terrible happenings new wonders of goodness and grace. Surround us with a sense of your present love. Grant your comfort and strength to the Mathias family that they may find comfort in you. We pray for those who now stand accused of this crime. If they are innocent, let that be clearly shown. If they are guilty, may they seek peace and reconciliation with you. We pray in the name of Jesus Christ who was dead, but lives and rules this world with you. Amen."

Holiday Blues

Anyone who has lived through a cycle of holidays after the loss of a loved one knows how difficult it can be. Loss, whether of a person, a building, a home, or a dream, hits with full force when we are faced with a world full of "happy" people. The Mathias murders came ten days before Christmas. One elder went home and took down the family Christmas tree the morning after the murders were discovered. Christmas Eve worship attendance that year reached an all-time low. People had been to church several times since the murders. How could they face the emotion of holiday services?

The staff of Northminster did a remarkable job of helping people address their conflicted feelings. They assured parishioners that Christmas was all about joy coming in the brokenness of the world. They prepared people for the unexpected shifts of feeling joyful and then despondent. Families with children were encouraged to celebrate with them as normally as possible. The services at the church, although a bit more somber than usual, were continued, and this wonderful, wounded community of faith ushered in the birth of the Christ child as best they could. When trauma strikes near a major church festival, that celebration will continue to be affected in the memory of those who lived through it. Like all memory, however, it will find its proper place in the heart of the congregation if the grief and recovery process is managed well.

Healing for Healers

Last, we need to remember the importance of worship for those who are "in the trenches" offering pastoral care and guidance during the crisis times. Often these individuals are expected to lead others in worship and to put their own need for spiritual healing on hold. Consider granting special time away to pastors or staff members three to six months after the trauma. Whether they spend their time in personal retreat or use it for rest, relaxation, and an opportunity to worship elsewhere where they're not leading, it can be restorative to their souls.

Michael Fletcher-Taylor told me that on a trip to North Carolina after the Oklahoma City bombing he worshipped in a congregation in Asheville. When worshippers learned that he had been involved in the relief efforts, they acknowledged him in worship and offered prayer for him and all those affected. Michael found himself suddenly aware of how much he had needed the experience of the community of believers holding him up.

Gale Izard told a similar experience of meeting a Jewish newspaperman in the airport at Tel Aviv several weeks after the bombing. Upon learning that the group was from Oklahoma City, this man, looking like an Old Testament prophet, threw his hands in the air and began to sob, "I'm so sorry, I'm so sorry, I have been praying for you." Again, this man's faith deeply ministered to one who had spent much energy ministering to others.

Worship is the heart of Christian life. Using the experience of being together in the presence of God for prayer, to hear the Word preached, to share at Christ's table, and to lay out all our emotions is one of the most effective ways of helping a congregation to cope with the reality of what has happened. Worship is God's gift to us as well as our gift to God.

CHAPTER 7

Surviving in the Public Eye

What we see, read, hear and sing along to, dear God, has numbed us like Novocaine in a jaw. We can't feel the drilling of our own sensitivities or hear the cries of those who need us. We are shock-proof from an overload of violence and doomsayers.

> —Margaret Anne Huffman,
> *"Through the Valley..." Prayers for Violent Times*, p. 80

Roman Catholics all over Indiana were dumbfounded when they glimpsed the front page of the *Indianapolis Star* on Sunday morning, February 16, 1997. There, beneath bold headlines, was an appalling account of the alleged sexual misconduct of priests in the Lafayette Diocese. The three-day series of exposé articles titled "Faith Betrayed" was written by investigative reporters Linda Graham Caleca and Richard Walton.[1] The articles named names and pointed fingers— especially at the bishop of Lafayette, who, although he had disciplined many of the accused, was criticized for having done so quietly and without sharing information with congregants. The artwork accompanying the front-page article showed a child looking down. The reader could observe the long arms of a faceless man in a clerical collar reaching down her shoulders. The caption said, "Trusting young victims, all easy prey."

The articles reported that in the past 25 years, 16 current and former priests had been accused of sexual misconduct with minors of both sexes, ranging from young children to adolescents. The *Star* further indicated that the diocese had admitted to 12 alleged incidents of sexual misconduct by priests, with 40 victims having stepped forward over the past 12 years. The *Star* later revealed that it had received more than 400 responses from readers to the series.[2] Comments ranged from one by a woman who said she was offended at seeing the stories "splashed" across the front page to accolades for the series from readers who were appalled at the church's lack of responsiveness to these issues. According to one priest who requested anonymity, "It's the silence that gets to us . . . why doesn't the Diocese just say something?"

Today the diocese remains silent, fighting the lawsuits that have arisen over many of the allegations. In a telephone interview, an outspoken priest who had criticized the bishop for not following his own policies reminded me that the focus of the articles was not on revealing the truth of the incidents but on bringing to public awareness that victims were hurting. Many felt their needs had not been met by the church they loved so dearly. Today the Lafayette Diocese remains divided over these issues, with priests and lay leaders choosing sides. The series' goal of addressing these hurts has yet to be met. Instead, issues of protection, denial, and trust remain at the heart of many congregants and priests alike.

Such journalism is an example of what traumatized congregations face. Sometimes the trauma results from the news coverage, as was the case with the "Faith Betrayed" series. At other times, the coverage merely escalates existing emotions or reopens difficult memories. There is a fine line between the public's right to know and the possible damage done by the ripples that spread from public awareness. Mental-health professionals refer to such trauma as secondary victimization.[3]

Another investigative story was broken on the front page of the *Star* on Sunday, June 15, 1997, under the headline "The Mathias Murders— Police Have a Prime Suspect But Not Enough Evidence to Arrest Him."[4] This article disclosed that a primary suspect in the murder was a 14-year-old member of the congregation, a young man who had been troublesome but active in the church. This lead article filled page six with revealing details of the investigation previously unknown to the majority of the congregation. A "sidebar" piece highlighted Northminster's journey of the last six months with a photo of the church's memory board.

Mark Moore, spokesperson for Northminster, knew the article was coming. "We tried to encourage the writer not to be so forthright but were unsuccessful. He believed that the public had the right to know and that, in fact, revealing so much might help someone with information come forward." The police agreed. Any pressure and a continued high public profile might help the case. Not all members of Northminster shared this opinion. For many, the publication of this story marked the first time they had seriously considered that this shocking act of violence might have been perpetrated by one of their own. They now had to integrate into their thinking such questions as "Who is it? Do I know this person? Are we safe?" Northminster's summer schedule included only one weekly worship service. On that Sunday morning parishioners and visitors were invited to remain after the benediction for a discussion of the article led by Mark Moore. Many, but not all, stayed.

Our country is entertained by the spectacle of trauma—especially when it involves crime. We are riveted to the television for our favorite police or attorney drama. We tape our favorite TV hospital series when we have a Thursday night meeting. Murder mysteries, disaster films, and true-life crime books are in demand as eager consumers seek to be titillated. U.S. prime-time television targeted mainly to adults offers an average of five violent acts per hour, with children's cartoons portraying 26 violent acts per hour.[5] Lula Redmond, a therapist who specializes in the treatment of families of murder victims, writes:

> As a nation, we are intrigued with the mystique of these pathological activities. The media makes these stories commercially viable and we watch. The virus of information spreads, which may not only be infectious but psychologically damaging. The tendency is to glamorize crime and the criminal, and to degrade the profiles of victims. The press cannot be sued for libel by the dead. [6]

Many trauma victims or survivors indicate that they can never watch the news or read a novel again with the same cavalier attitude. We cannot blame the press or the media alone. We are willing participants.

The Press

In an interview with Judith Cebula,[7] religion writer at the *Indianapolis Star,* I asked, "Why do newspapers sometimes print things that are disruptive to congregational life and seem to add to the existing trauma?"

As previously mentioned, the newspaper sees itself as having an obligation to inform the public. Part of this responsibility is to monitor civil servants and agencies such as the police department that are funded by taxpayer dollars. Newspapers cover the community and, as a part of the public concern, carefully watch police reports, court activity, and government functioning.

"Crime reporting is the bedrock of what papers do," Judith explained. "They seek to respond to the questions of the public—Are we safe? What actually happened? Did all officials act promptly and correctly? Those who determine what articles will be pursued often ask themselves what the readers want to know, what are the things they are thinking about." This concern for reader interest explains many of the human-interest stories that emerge after a disaster or tragedy, as well as the reporting that we may label shocking. In the end, the responsibility to the public is viewed as greater than sensitivity to any particular victim or situation.

How Newspapers Work

It can be helpful to understand the organization of a newspaper and how decisions are made. The operation of each paper is unique. In smaller communities one or two people may do everything. On a city paper the hierarchy will involve several types of reporters and several levels of decision-making. Editors and assistant editors generally oversee each major area. These editors work with reporters who have different roles. Beat reporters work only one content area, such as sports or religion. Feature writers prepare special stories on a variety of subjects but may have a particular focus or expertise. Investigative reporting involves staff who may work in one area doing research for a series of explosive news stories or exposés. These writers differ from the daily crime reporters; investigative assignments sometimes extend over a period of months. General-assignment reporters are "floaters" who work where needed, often on weekends. When a story breaks, editors may or may not consult with one another. The handling of a story often depends on where and when the story breaks.

In the reporting of traumatic incidents, it is not uncommon to see "layers" of coverage with several writers generating different perspectives on the newsworthy event. An example is the Mathias murder coverage. Since the murders occurred on a Sunday evening, they were initially covered by a night police reporter. The follow-up story that appeared Tuesday was handled by a day police reporter with a totally different writing style. Three months later a "lingering mystery story" was published as Northminster celebrated its first Easter after the murders. It was written by a general-assignment reporter at the recommendation of the religion writer. The June 15 article noted earlier was written by a project writer in an investigative style.

The relationship between the editor and the reporter is unique. Getting to know a particular reporter may be helpful, but reporters can only lobby their editors. The editor has the final say on what stories are researched and how assignments are made, and determines the final focus and text.

"Off the record" is a term most of us hear in the movies. In real life it means the reporter will not attribute the information directly to the source. It does not mean that the reporter will not research the situation or detail in an attempt to document it from other sources. Once you've said it and the reporter has heard it, it's fair game. Therefore, if you're the only possible source of the information and want to be certain that it's not shared, be careful about speaking "off the record." Reporters will generally not allow a source to see a story before it is published. They contend that they can't release the story before it's run, or they will find themselves constantly arguing with sources over slant and content. Giving veto power to a source compromises the right of free expression of the press, reporters say. Many will, however, read back quotes to a source to ensure accuracy. Since people are usually anxious when being interviewed, it's a good idea to leave the door open with the reporter for verification of information.

Working with the Press

Press conferences are generally boring to newspapers, and they often send second-level staff to cover them. Written statements can, however, be helpful. The press, like other media, is interested in the human-interest angle. Having people ready to be interviewed who reflect a wide range of experience and emotional response is a good idea. Choose your most articulate representatives for this role. Deadlines will be discussed in the section on the electronic media, but they are just as crucial for newspapers. If your interviewee isn't available on the newspaper's timeline, have a backup ready.

The conclusions I can draw about working with the press are these:

1. Even though the trauma may involve a religious organization, it is unlikely that it will be covered initially by a religion specialist.

2. You should expect that a number of reporters will be working on your story, not just one.

3. Be aware that different divisions of the newspaper will take different approaches in their writing.

4. When negotiating with reporters, remember that they have varying degrees of authority on what they can and cannot promise you.

5. Don't discuss anything you don't want to see in print. "Off the record" means only that your name isn't attached to the information.

6. Express a willingness to be available to verify the accuracy of quotes.

7. You may help arrange photographic sessions and establish rules for the presence of photographers in worship.

8. Press conferences are of limited interest, but written statements and arranged interviews are helpful.

Judith Cebula suggested that one of the best strategies is to make friends with the press before you encounter reporters in a crisis. Build a positive relationship with at least one person on the newspaper staff who can help you get to know the ropes of the paper's system of news coverage. In larger cities the place to start may be with the religion department.[8]

Interviews and Spokespeople

Earlier chapters referred to the congregation's "spokesperson." If at all possible, such a person should have previous experience in dealing with the press and media. If no one with this background is available, it is important to help the person selected understand the needs of the press and media. Because of deadlines and competition, getting the news out quickly is imperative for both newspapers and television. It is easy to misunderstand the behavior of a reporter under the pressure of obtaining timely information. Sometimes a manner perceived as impatient or aggressive actually reflects the reporter's urgency to get to the heart of the matter quickly.[9] Here are some things to remember for both print and media interviews:

1. Give short, clear, and concise answers to questions.

2. If you do not understand the question, ask the interviewer to repeat it.

3. Remain calm and rational, even if the reporter appears to be baiting.

4. If the interviewer appears hostile, the best approach is to use humility or, if appropriate, humor.

5. Try to be as relaxed and informal as possible.

6. If negative questions are anticipated, rehearse responses in advance and focus on the positive points.

7. Be sincere and tell the truth.

8. Remember that "no comment" invites the reporter to look elsewhere for answers. It's better to respond and to have some control over what is said.

9. If the interview is being taped and an opposing viewpoint is to be represented, you may wish to suggest a person rather than leaving it to random choice.

10. Ask about the deadline. If it's for a televised newscast, at what hour will it be shown? If it's a feature article or magazine interview, you may have time to gather additional information.

11. Determine ahead of time if you'll respond to questions. Then stick to your decision.

12. Make multiple copies of background information sheets about the church and relevant individuals to distribute to press and media. Supplying such facts ensures accurate information.

13. Remember that the media really don't enjoy press conferences. Many times, television reporters won't show because there's little to film that's of interest. If you choose to hold a press conference, schedule it in the morning, not at 4:00 P.M. when reporters are tired, close to deadline, and under editing pressure.

It is important to realize that if people feel that their privacy rights have been violated, there may be little to be done. Generally legal action against the media in news-related incidents is unsuccessful. It may be better simply to keep in mind these "rights" which you take charge of yourself:

1. You can say "no" to any interview.

2. You can refuse one reporter even though you've agreed to speak to another.

3. You can exclude children from interviews.

4. You can refuse to answer any question asked you.

5. You can demand a correction if information is inaccurately reported.

6. You can request that a silhouette be used in a television interview.

7. You can ask that offensive photographs or visuals be omitted from a report.

8. You can file a formal complaint against any reporter.[10]

Television

"If you don't feed the beast, it'll feed on you." Thus began my interview with Rich Van Wyck, news reporter for WTHR-TV, the NBC affiliate in Indianapolis. Rich, an elder at Fairview Presbyterian Church, is frequently on the scene of major traumas throughout the state of Indiana and has a wealth of experience in conducting live interviews.

By 1987, 98 percent of all homes in the United States had at least one television and 68 percent had more than one. Sixty-six percent of respondents polled from the general public stated that they got their news mainly from TV, and 50 percent believed it was the most reliable source of news.[11] Van Wyck reminded me that the news that people used to receive once a day in the morning paper they now get at 6:00 A.M., 1:00 P.M., and again at 5:00, 5:30, 6:00, and 11:00 P.M. (eastern time). Each reporting cycle takes a slightly different angle on any story. Television reporting is an ongoing process.[12]

When dealing with television coverage it's important to know whether it is live or videotaped. The choice will often depend on the time of day and the degree of seriousness or interest surrounding the event. Since most of the facts can be verified by the officials involved, most media reporters are looking for reactions. Television wants to know what the "average" person in the pew is experiencing. That's why you so see so many neighbors or friends of victims interviewed. Since the electronic media are image-dominant, it's a good idea to vary the people you provide for interviews by age, gender, race, and role. Extended interviews are generally edited to only a few minutes—or seconds —unless they are part of a news "talk show." In a brief interview only one or two prime points can be made. In media terms these are called "Single Overriding Communications Objectives" (SOCO). A person to be interviewed should decide on the SOCOs in advance and mentally rehearse them so they can be comfortably included in the interview.

Cameras in Church

Whether to allow cameras in church is always a difficult decision. Generally speaking, it is better to agree to taping than to deny the request. Remember, a telecast can also be an opportunity to witness to God's healing power, one that will reach many more people than just those gathered for the worship service. Some things to remember when dealing with film crews in worship:

1. Most television stations will want to be represented by their own film crew.

2. You can limit the number of crews and insist that they "pool" the tape. Some stations will resist your decision, but it can generally be negotiated with effort.

3. You should also ask for stable cameras on tripods during worship services rather than roving cameras.

4. Request that TV crews use no additional lighting.

5. Plan to be present at least a half-hour early to monitor film activity.

6. You may request that reporters not approach worshippers or leaders for comments or interviews inside the church. Again, it's helpful to invite the press to a common space after the service where you can provide a variety of people with whom reporters can speak.

7. A little kindness goes a long way. Most media reporters are not greeted warmly. If you offer a hospitable presence, they are likely to be more gentle.

I asked Rich to comment on congregational trauma that involves something the pastor has done or is accused of doing, or a situation when the church is held at fault for some trauma. He recommended that it is still better to give a concerned, general statement and provide people to be interviewed rather than to remain silent. If attorneys are involved, they will wish to speak on behalf of the church, but you can be sure that the media will look for other people to talk—and with proven success! Therefore, proactive statements are most helpful. An attorney can coach the spokespeople, but indisputable facts are generally the best: "Our pastor, _____, has been charged with _____ , and we are all concerned that justice and fairness prevail for all involved. We are praying for a clear and prompt resolution to this situation."

Church members can take an adverse situation and make themselves look caring and responsible by the way they handle it. Later, they may need the media to help balance the image of the congregation or to put a positive "spin" on the situation. Alienating the media in the early days of an unfolding drama could be costly later. Naturally, if attorneys are involved because of the nature of the trauma, church leadership should be counseled carefully on implementing these suggestions. Rich Van Wyck also suggested that in some situations it may be to the church's advantage to consult a public-relations firm to assist in image recovery following an embarrassing event.

Coverage Can Help

Lest the reader think that media coverage is an ordeal to be feared, consider that it can have a powerful role in the healing of a community. Many TV and radio stations are open to providing community programming after major traumas. Special programs to assist parents, programs targeted to children, or programs on religious stations that address the larger issues of faith raised by trauma can all be part of the corporate healing of a community. Television, radio, and newspapers are also the quickest and most effective ways of notifying the public of special services, funds, and events in which the community may wish to participate. We can tame the beast and make it our friend. To do so means recognizing both the individual and mutual goals of the church and the media. It takes some work, but it's worth it in the end.

Law Enforcement Agencies

Most of us experience police officers as the men and women in blue who give us traffic tickets. When police officers or sheriffs are involved with a crime that affects us, they take on a different appearance. The relationship may begin shifting with the news that something terrible has happened. Janice Harris Lord, director of victim services for Mothers Against Drunk Driving national headquarters, has provided law-enforcement organizations with outlines and training for delivering the devastating news that a loved one has been harmed.

However, Lord says, "No matter how the message is conveyed, the memories of those moments will be etched in the mind of the survivors forever. Surviving family members frequently remember the exact words used, how the officer looked, the number on the police badge, the way one stood or even held their hat."[13] The officer bearing the news will often bring along a police chaplain who can remain with the family to review the information known and to help in the immediate shock response. The chaplain's role can be critical, since survivors may not have understood the news or be able to accept it. Law-enforcement chaplains have received special training to help them in these circumstances. It is important to remember that law-enforcement personnel have very difficult jobs. Sometimes the "tough" exterior and the seeming inability to show emotion are a way of coping with the demands of the job.

It is important to realize that a variety of officers may relate to a particular situation. A beat officer may initially be called to the crime scene, followed later by detectives or a team of investigators. Generally, as the law-enforcement strategy for handling the crime is determined, a church can expect to deal with one or possibly two officers as time goes on. If we are the survivors or victims of the crime, we will likely perceive these individuals as friends. If, however, the church has been the site of criminal activity, we may feel that the police are being insensitive to our embarrassment or concerns.

Be aware that the police have a job to do. This job may make us feel uncomfortable, but we need to cooperate if the truth is to be discovered. If you are uncomfortable responding to police questions, you have the right to ask an attorney to be present for any interviews, even if you are not being accused of a crime. The officer's role doesn't end with an arrest. He or she is often asked to testify for the prosecution through appearances at grand jury hearings or preliminary hearings, or as a witness at the trial.

Officers as Resource People

It is appropriate and at times desirable to ask representatives of the law-enforcement team to speak to the congregation and staff. This meeting can be especially helpful during an ongoing investigation. Police are also willing to assist the congregation in evaluating the church's current security system. Police department chaplains can be of great help in explaining procedures during this time. Northminster's experience with the Marion County Sheriff's Department during the Mathias murder investigation was positive. Investigating officers were open to receiving calls and responding to our questions. We received periodic updates from the sheriff's department during the 13-month investigation. Individuals should not be intimidated by asking questions of the police. You can be certain they will not tell you anything you should not know!

Rewards

Whether to offer a reward was a topic debated in the Northminster situation. The police explained that rewards can be useful in motivating certain types of people to come forward with information, but rewards also draw many false leads. Individuals in a congregation may wish to contribute toward a reward fund. It should be up to the congregation's decision-making body to decide whether such a fund is formally sponsored by the church. Northminster did install a "tip" line where information about the crime could be left on a secure telephone line. Such information was then forwarded to the police department for follow-up.

Understanding the Criminal Justice System

If the trauma leads to an encounter with the criminal justice system, I strongly recommend that an attorney in the church take on the role of "interpreter" of the process. Terms like plea bargains, continuance, court reporters, and pretrials are understood in the context of television but can become confusing for the person not familiar with the ins and outs of our legal system.

The American criminal justice system differs in a significant way from that of its parent system in England. In our nation, crimes are committed against the state, not against the individual. If the victim is living, that person is treated as a witness to the crime. This is only one example of why our criminal justice system can be overwhelming, confusing, and intimidating. When we are the accused, we often view the system as leaning toward the side of our accusers. When we are the victim, we see it bending over backward to protect the accused. Either way, it is stressful to participate in legal proceedings. The justice system can be compartmentalized into four stages: law enforcement, prosecution, judiciary proceeding, and corrections.[14] Having previously discussed law enforcement, I will now look briefly at the other three components of the criminal-justice system.

The prosecutorial phase is the point at which many of the rights of the accused and those of the victim interact with each other. The right to legal representation (private or through a public defender), the right to a speedy trial, the right to be informed about the proceedings, and the right to be heard are guaranteed in every court only to the alleged offender. Most systems will work hard, however, to assure these rights for victims too. To date 29 states have passed constitutional amendments to guarantee the rights of crime victims. A 1990 National Assessment Program survey of state and local jurisdictions sponsored by the National Institute of Justice found that 86 percent of prosecutors' offices also had some form of victim/witness assistance program. If such is available, the prosecutor's office will assign a victim assistance advocate to work with the survivors or victims. The advocate will offer a range of services but will also be readily available to explain each step of the process.

In the judiciary phase of the system, a judge oversees court proceedings. The judge ensures that the law is followed and makes the final decision or ruling at each stage. The judge will determine the release status of an alleged offender, decide whether or not to accept a guilty plea or a negotiated plea, preside over the trial, and determine the sentence, although there may be a sentencing recommendation from the jury. The 1982 President's Task Force on Victims of Crime made several recommendations to the judiciary. These include allowing victims and witnesses to be on call for the court proceedings; providing separate waiting rooms away from the defense witnesses or the defendant's family; considering the interests of the harmed when ruling on case continuances which draw out the process even longer; allowing written and oral victim-impact statements at sentencing hearings; and ordering restitution in cases when the victim has suffered a financial loss. Many judges follow these recommendations closely, although they are not legally bound to do so.

The corrections phase of the process describes either the institutional supervision (incarceration) or the community supervision (probation) when a guilty verdict has been rendered. A person who is incarcerated becomes the complete responsibility of the state. If probation is used as an alternative, the person may be supervised directly by the court (court probation) or by a probation officer from the community or state corrections division. Probation is generally used only when the person is not considered a threat to society. If a person convicted of a crime is released early on parole, the corrections facility should take responsibility for notifying the victims or survivors about the inmate's status and upcoming release. Some states have instituted laws to this effect. It is important to know the laws in your state in regard to early parole reporting.[15]

Attending Trials

In many instances it is important for those most directly affected by the crime to attend the trial. Their presence is one way for people to see that the victims and survivors are important to society. It can, in many instances, contribute to the healing process. For some, attending the trial renews a sense of control and may help the grieving person feel that he or she is "representing" the injured loved one.[16] If members of the staff or congregation plan on attending the trial, it can be helpful to prepare. An excellent resource is *Victims: A Manual for Clergy and Congregations,* available through The Spiritual Dimension in Victim Services, an organization formed to raise awareness of the spiritual crisis victims often experience. Among the reminders included:

1. If victims or survivors attending the trial appear to be fueled by revenge, they may be put at arm's length in the process or misrepresented by the press.

2. When an arrest is made, there is an immediate sense of relief. Unfortunately, we must be reminded that arrests do not necessarily lead to prosecutions, or prosecutions to convictions, or convictions to stiff sentences, or stiff sentences to stiff sentences served.

3. Cases may be continued over and over again before they go to trial. They can be delayed for months or even years. The appellate process can extend the time frame even longer.

4. Unless the case is heard in a state that has passed a "court atten-
    dance" act, the survivors may be barred from attending the pro-
    ceeding because it could be viewed as prejudicial to the jury.

5. Plea bargains may result in lesser charges. This outcome can lead to
    disillusionment.

6. The verdict may not reflect the survivors' sense of justice.

7. The sense of relief that an arrest has been made and a verdict
    rendered can put grief on hold. When the trial is over, the people
    most affected may step back into the grief and be surprised that it's
    not finished.[17]

Pastoral care during the trial is important for all involved. Legal
interpretations or rationales for why many things happen may be available, but these do little to alleviate the human emotions of frustration and
anger.

Individuals attending trials need to remember that they are still in
the public eye. Although they may refuse media interviews, they cannot
keep themselves from being photographed or filmed. A police escort can
be made available to take people to and from the proceedings.

The religious community continued to play an important role in the
response to victims, survivors, and their families in the Oklahoma bombing incident. "Safe Haven," whose work is described below, was a program developed through the efforts of area ecumenical groups. Its leadership included United Methodist, Presbyterian, and Roman Catholic
representatives, as well as an official from Project Heartland, the
FEMA-funded counseling agency. The U.S. Attorney's office made
provisions for any survivor or victim's family member who wished to
attend to be present for a portion of one of the two trials held in Denver.
The attendance order was determined by a lottery. "Safe Havens" were
organized outside the courtroom in Denver and outside the closed-circuit telecast in Oklahoma City.

Various religious groups pooled their funds through the Resource
Coordinating Committee to provide day care or child care of the parents'
choice for those wishing to attend a trial either at one of the Denver sites
or at Safe Haven in Oklahoma City. The Oklahoma City broadcast site

was on federal property and was treated as a courtroom. Safe Haven was allowed to place two professional volunteers in both courtrooms. These individuals were trained to help with emotional needs, should the testimonies become overwhelming to those present. Three hundred volunteers were trained to work half-day shifts at the Safe Haven sites. These volunteers included laypeople, clergy, and mental-health workers. Chaplains were available throughout the trial for those needing help.

In smaller trial settings, it should also be assumed that although not every member of a congregation will attend a trial, most will follow it closely through news accounts. Extra effort should be put forth to ensure that pastoral care or counseling is available through both formal and informal means. A "debriefing" for those attending the trial, similar to that offered chaplains, may be a helpful way of dealing with the events of the day.

In the end, we must stay focused on the difference between retribution and restoration. Retribution returns evil for evil, chaos for chaos, and is revenge-motivated. Restoration seeks to bring order out of chaos and is justice-motivated. Retribution is energy-draining because it continues to focus on hate or the inability to forgive. Restoration moves beyond condemnation yet at the same time does not condone the wrong. It is energizing because it stops corrosive attitudes and additional victimization, allowing the healing to continue.[18] The church needs to promote restoration, even when it is difficult to do so.

The public eye is not comfortable. With God's help and careful planning, a congregation can use this spotlight as a witness to the power of God to heal and make whole even the most atrocious events. Even our public pain can be a tool for Christ.

CHAPTER 8

Who Will Help?
The Role of the Outside
Consultant

In this dark, mean-minded world of ours, God, we are wandering
around like kids lost in a cave. Touched by violence, personal or
random, we inch perilously close to the edge of despair, unable to
see where we are going. Send us guides who've traveled dark
passages before; send us pathfinders.

—Margaret Anne Huffman,
"Through the Valley..." Prayers for Violent Times, p. 141

Most readers of this book are helpers. You may be a judicatory staff
member, a pastor, a member of a congregation, or a professional church
consultant. Whatever the formal role, you likely see yourself as someone
who can assist a congregation recovering from trauma. It is important for
hurting churches to have such support from outside their membership.

Doing Your Own Homework First

One of the most important things for helpers to know is their own response to trauma. Understanding one's own reaction to death, destruction,
and loss is of paramount importance. Without this knowledge, attempts
to help may be sabotaged by the unconscious psychological issues opera-
tive in the mind and heart of the helper. Just as congregations have patterns that have been developed over years, so individuals have learned
how to cope with and respond to trauma through their family of origin
and their own life experiences. A person may be very effective helping

in one situation and totally unable to function in another. Self-knowledge is essential in regard to what types of trauma one can handle and what traumas trigger personal issues. The fine balance between these two is not easy to master unless we know ourselves well. There are always individuals who can help. We cannot assume that we're right for every job. It's a good idea to know others in your area and your denomination to whom you may refer those torn by trauma.

The Role of the Outside Helper

The outside helper's first task is to assist in bringing stability out of the chaos that results from trauma. Naturally, circumstance will determine exactly what must be done. Sometimes the helper is a "coach" like American Baptist official Riley Walker in the first hours after the news broke of Marty Travelstead's death. Sometimes the helper becomes the "leader," as I did in the first hours following the Mathias murders. Almost always, the outside person helps to determine what immediate steps should be taken in bringing order to the situation. The helper is another level head in sorting through the rubble, whether literal or figurative. Helpers may or may not be professionals in the mental health field. The most important factors are that they be caring and sensitive, and that they be good listeners. They are generally not part of the congregation experiencing the crisis. They may be judicatory staff or individuals recommended by the judicatory. It is important for the helper to respect lines of authority that exist in the situation but also to provide concrete suggestions or direction about next steps.

The helper needs to be a calm presence. If you have arrived early at the scene, ask two different people what has happened. This approach helps to calm others as the retelling focuses their thoughts. It also allows you to compare stories and perspectives on what the situation entails. Listen carefully for what is missing in these accounts.

If your role is not clear, ask others how you can be of help. Let them know what you can and cannot do. Offer to call others to assist. Watch carefully to see what role is not being played, and step into it if necessary. Remember that the first hours are often a "free-for-all" time, as were the early hours following the Oklahoma City bombing. Things will begin settling down as the initial shock is absorbed.

The helper's second task may be to link the congregation with other needed resources. Again, prior knowledge of the community is invaluable. In some denominations a team will be assigned to work with the church past the first days of the trauma. In disaster situations, resources will be made available through FEMA, Church World Service, and denominationally related programs.

The third general task is follow-up. Often the church gets extensive support during the first stages of the trauma, only to face the long haul without it. Maintaining contact with the church through the first year of the trauma is important to provide the secure base of support needed. It is important, however, that the congregation not become dependent on outside helpers. The goal should be to enable the congregation ultimately to cope on its own. People and congregations recover best when allowed to return to their own internal support systems and to experience a sense of control, meaning, and emotional respite.[1] For this reason, more involvement occurs at the beginning of the trauma and, as the congregation gradually rebuilds its strength, help is slowly withdrawn.

The fourth task is that of "cheerleader." It is important for the helper not only to comment on the shared pain but also to commend the courage, pride, and support of the community.[2] People get stronger by hearing that they are doing a good job, that they're coping, that we're amazed at how well they are handling the situation (if indeed we are amazed). Affirmation is as important in trauma as in any human saga. Letting the congregation know that we see healing and progress is definitely part of the outside helper's role.

The final task is closure on the helping relationship. Support from the outside should stay in place as long as needed. When, however, the healing time is well along the way and all indicators suggest that the helper's presence is no longer needed, one should withdraw. This move protects the helper from overinvolvement and the congregation from extended dependency. A period of evaluation and reflection with congregational decision-makers can help formalize this closure. This ending is important for any outside helper who has worked with the church beyond the first week or so of the traumatic event.

A Note to Denominational Executives

If you are a denominational executive or bishop, your role as an "outside" helper is especially important. You may not be the constant helping presence during the recovery period, but your ongoing care and concern need to be felt by all involved.

Only a denominational executive could say this to her colleagues: We are the servants in these situations, not the stars. Although we may be called upon to speak to the media or the press, our focus is always on the unfolding trauma. It is never a "photo op" or a chance to be perceived as the one in charge. If we have the skills to help, we should. If we don't have the necessary skills, we should be sure that someone who does is present and we should stay out of the way! These words may sound harsh, but I received too many reports in my research indicating that well-meaning staff could become more taxing than helpful. Most of us are called to be pastors to pastors or administrators, not to be specialists in trauma. On the other hand, the role of the judicatory executive or bishop is important to the life of the church affected and to the larger judicatory. We should be present in appropriate settings, and we should be present frequently during the healing process. Our role may be only to offer a prayer or to worship with the healing community, but we need to stay in touch with the situation long after the lights of the cameras have dimmed.

A Note to Interim Pastors

If you are an interim pastor seeking to fulfill the helper role by serving as a transitional shepherd, get all the training you can. The ministry of healing a traumatized church is very different from either the regular tasks of an interim period or the special needs of a highly conflicted church. The interim period following a trauma is likely to be longer and more challenging than any other interim setting.

If you are new to the community, ask other pastors to familiarize you with the resources available. Talk with judicatory officials about the history of the congregation. Clues to caring for this body are lodged in its history as a church.

You may wish to join a support or case-study group with other interim pastors. They can serve as sounding boards for your progress in ministering to the healing congregation. If you had a coach or mentor in your interim training, consider contracting with that person for regular consultation, even if only by telephone.

A Note to Members of a Traumatized Church

If you are a member of a traumatized church, your leadership and skill will be helpful to your congregation during this time. Remember, however, that you cannot be the primary helper and also do your own recovery homework. The members of Northminster Presbyterian who served on the care team were members of the helping professions. They wisely knew, however, that they could not be the ones to deliver the help. They planned the care, made certain the right leadership from outside was recruited to offer it, and interpreted the care available to the congregation. They also sought the help they needed for their own healing. You can help your church by seeing that something similar occurs there. Later, your experiences may be invaluable to others. You may be able to organize a response team in your community or in your judicatory. You may be called upon to serve as an "outside helper" to another congregation during a time of trauma.

A Final Word on Helping

Remember that the best way to be a helper is to be prepared. Know your local resources—counselors, law-enforcement officials, hospital and funeral-home workers, the local chapter of the American Red Cross, and other agencies. Learn the disaster plan for your community. Keep yourself spiritually and emotionally fit so that you'll be able to serve when called upon.

Finally, remember that each situation is unique and that no pat program will fit all settings. The suggestions in this book are examples intended to stimulate the reader's own thinking. Modify, create, and recycle any idea that will help in the situation that you face. Don't get in over your head: Ask for help when you need it. Most important, remember that each trauma is ultimately in God's hands. We are instruments of God's healing, the hands and feet of Christ in the world. It is a humbling, awesome responsibility. With God's help, we can do it.

CHAPTER 9

Moving Toward Wholeness

> *Pull us to our feet; gently nudge us onto the dance floor of life, tap out a sprightly beat to get us moving. Remind us that our strength is your joy. Play the music louder as we accept our places among the grace-full dancers.*
>
> —Margaret Anne Huffman,
> *"Through the Valley..." Prayers for Violent Times,* p. 175

Fortunately, trauma does not go on forever. God has built within the human heart a remarkable capacity for resilience. Author Charles Olsen says:

> Congregations which have a sense of story or journey and an awareness that God is a player with a role in the story tend to be congregations of vital faith. New people who visit them immediately pick that up and are attracted to it. They observe a natural witness that grows out of the church's life and reflections about their story. Conversely, congregations which have no sense of story or journey and no awareness of God being a player with a role in their stories, tend to be congregations of lethargic faith. New people who visit them pick that up as well and are not attracted.[1]

Congregations that have been affected by trauma must rewrite their story. How will they tell this tale? How will they integrate what has happened to them into the way they understand their mission in the world? The story of a congregation's journey through pain and sorrow permanently changes its understanding of God, itself, and the world in which it lives. The steps members take to move the story beyond trauma and into God's redemptive plan for all of creation will be a significant determinant in their future.

Rebuilding Our Image

The fear that no one will ever want to join the church again is on the minds of most members in a church where the trauma stemmed from crime or violence. Churches traumatized by the misconduct of pastors or key leaders fear that trust can never be reestablished. Communities of faith affected by disasters may think that the challenge is to rebuild the building bigger and better as a way of saying, "We're okay!" In the end, the questions are the same: Will we ever get over this? Will people ever want to join our church again?

The answer lies in our trust that Christ's victory for us has overcome every obstacle and therefore we, too, can share in a future of promise. No matter what has happened, God can turn our mourning into dancing; those who see our joy, even in the aftermath of trauma, may say, "I want to be a part of that too."

Mary Susan Gast puts it beautifully when she says, "We have hope! We remember the story that new life came out of a death that grew out of love. And we live with hope that far beyond the horizon of our wisdom, a new reality is taking shape that will astound us. We cherish the hope that, although it is shrouded in shadow, dawn is ready to shimmer forth and reveal a new heaven, a new earth."[2]

Reflecting on Our Story

Having done the hard work of grieving, after at least the first anniversary, the church may be ready to step out into this hope we cherish so dearly. Return to chapter five and review the six points of identification used by Northminster to assess its healing. Where are these in the life of your congregation? Also discuss the following questions:

1. How has God's presence made a difference in our journey? In what moments have we felt God's presence most clearly? Where in the

story did something happen that could be attributed only to "the hand of God"?

2. How has this chapter in our story made us more sensitive to others in pain? As Fay Angus describes it, "In the valleys of our sorrows and our griefs we cultivate . . . understanding, compassion, courage, sensitivity, sympathy, kindness and all those tender mercies."[3]

3. What special ministry might we be called to that grows out of our own experience of brokenness? Is a special ministry to victims of crime on our hearts? Perhaps our calling lies in a ministry with prisoners. Has the loss of a building in which to worship made us more aware of the plight of those who have nowhere to live? The congregation may hear a call to ministry with the homeless.

4. How have we become stronger as a congregation through this ordeal? How has the family of God drawn together to respond to the challenge of grief and loss? What gifts of leadership have arisen from those who normally sit on the sidelines?

When people are able and willing to reflect on these questions, healing is almost complete.

Where Are They Now?

The congregation of First Baptist Church in Shelbyville is now worshipping in its restored sanctuary. Members have celebrated their first Easter without the Rev. Marty Travelstead. It was hard, but they knew that Marty's life was a witness to the resurrection they celebrated. They trusted that the promise of the resurrection belongs to Marty as well as to them. In a letter of April 18, 1998, member Mark Mason said, "This tragedy taught me one thing. There are no big cogs. God takes care of us all. One cog can fall off of the gear and He keeps the gear turning. We are coming up on the anniversary of this tragedy. We have proven one thing: God will always be there for His people, and the First Baptist Church of Shelbyville, Indiana, will go on to do His work." That knowledge makes it easier.

As I complete this book, the churches of Oklahoma City have cy-cled past another anniversary of the bombing of the Alfred P. Murrah Federal Building. A new little chapel has been constructed across the street at the site of the makeshift morgue. Many visitors and residents alike will journey to the still barren lot where men, women, and children once felt safe at work and at play. There have been moments of silence and special prayers. For those who served as helpers during the trauma, the Guy Ameses and Steve Vinsons of the world, there was much to remember. In reviewing this manuscript, Tracey Evans reported that the Resource Coordinating Committee continues to meet every other week and, three years later, still hears stories of great need.

Almost two years after the murder of its pastor and his wife, Northminster Presbyterian Church is ready to begin the next chapter. The congregation still faces a series of criminal trials with uncertain outcomes, but they are not standing still waiting for the verdict. The session has entered into a multichurch study of the Presbyterian presence in the city of Indianapolis, believing they have a unique role in fulfilling unmet needs. A new outreach committee is focusing on attracting young families living in the neighborhood. There is talk of adding a contem-porary worship service with a more varied approach to music. A mission study will start in 1999; this is the first stage of preparing to search for a new pastor. The cover of Northminster's 1998 Holy Week mailer fea-tured a pencil drawing by Bryan Larson, age six. It shows a smiling Jesus on the cross with a bright red butterfly to his left. "Once, for all . . ." it reads. Inside the leaflet is a drawing of a boy who looks remarkably like the cover-art Jesus, reaching out to catch the butterfly. The message continues, "so that we might all live with hope for every tomorrow." Northminster understands the cross but reaches out for the butterfly of hope and new life.

"I consider that the sufferings of this present time are not worth comparing with the glory about to be revealed to us. For the creation waits with eager longing for the revealing of the children of God. . . . For in hope we were saved" (Rom. 8:18, 24).

In Closing

When congregations are ready to step out in faith, make new plans, and no longer refer to the tragedy as an obstacle or singular defining point, we can assume that the past has been put into perspective. This final stage of grief involves reorganization or acceptance. We begin timidly to explore new traditions, perhaps different from the style of the beloved pastor we lost. We change our goals. The old sanctuary couldn't allow for drama because the pews couldn't be moved. We reopen the day-care center, unafraid to say to the community, "All Child Care Providers Screened."

This does not mean that we ever forget. The choice, however, to tell our story as one with a tragic ending or one with a new beginning belongs to us. God will help us, but the work belongs to us. And all God's people say, "Amen!"

Northminster Congregational Care Team Goals and Objectives

(approved January 2, 1997)

GOALS

1. To provide resources and support for the congregation in managing grief, anger, and other emotions which naturally arise in situations of violent loss.

2. In consultation with staff, to anticipate theological issues or matters of faith which may need to be addressed.

3. To facilitate and monitor the healing process.

OBJECTIVES

1. Services to Young Children:
   a. Provide a resource person to assist parents in identifying signs of anxiety, etc., in their children.
   b. Provide ongoing support to the director of Christian education and Sunday school teachers on how to deal with issues that come up in children's programming regarding the deaths and the investigation.
   c. Assess grief/healing process to determine additional services.

2. Services to Youth:
   a. Provide special forum or group session in which questions of faith and theology can be discussed, using the seminary's pastoral counseling department as a resource.

    b.   Assess grief/healing process to determine additional services.

3.   Services to Adults—Adult Education:
    a.   Assist the adult education committee in offering an additional class this spring on the order of *When Bad Things Happen to Good People.*
    b.   Assess grief/healing process to determine additional services.

4.   Services to Adults—Grief Counseling:
    a.   Continue with regular six-week bereavement group beginning January 13, 1997.
    b.   Provide weekly "time to talk" gatherings for congregation beginning January 13, 1997.

5.   Services to Adults—Homebound:
    a.   Support the deacons in their visitations to homebound members by:
       • Providing current information to be shared.
       • Discussing with deacons how information can be shared.
       • Offering appropriate Scripture readings and other comforting readings to deacons to share with homebound members.
       • Offering to make visitations as needed.
    b.   Assess grief/healing process to determine additional services.

6.   Services to Adults—Information (entire team):
    a.   Plan response strategies for when arrests are made (spiritual, media, telephone tree) or if the investigation goes on indefinitely.
    b.   Determine goals for possible meetings with representatives of sheriff's office, prosecutor's office, and/or police chaplain, and facilitate these meetings as needed.
    c.   Keep congregation informed on ministerial search; i.e., facilitate Presbytery Committee on Congregational Care members' meeting with congregation.

7.   Services to Adults—Self-Care and Education:
    a.   Support the self-care and education of members through accurate, professional information that deals with issues relating to

grief and healing for families and individuals.
- Develop a bibliography of resources to be put in library.
- Write self-help information and/or book reviews for the *News and Views* each month.
- Develop a "grief/healing" shelf in the library.
- Add resources to library as needed.
b. Keep congregation informed through *News and Views* and parish notes of activities of care team.
c. Assess grief/healing process to determine additional services.

8. Services to Adults and Youth—Spiritual:
   a. Provide Sunday evening vespers during Lent from 5:30 to 6:00 P.M. in the chapel.
   b. Support an appropriate grief/healing sermon series when transitional head of staff arrives.
   c. Plan prayer service for the evening that arrests are made.
   d. Assess grief/healing process to determine additional services.

9. Services to Staff:
   a. Notify staff of session's decision regarding counseling services.
   b. Support continued group time with Kay Schrader [of St. Vincent Crisis Response Team] as needed.
   c. Assess grief/healing process to determine additional services.

The Care Team will look at 1997 in six-week blocks to determine the most appropriate services to offer during each six-week period. Feedback from the session and congregation is encouraged and is a necessary part of the Care Team's ongoing assessment effort.

Working with Youth in Crisis

When working with adolescents, adults should remember the following:

1. Don't fall apart. It's OK to shed some tears and to express anger or other feelings verbally so long as emotional control remains intact. The young person may reason that if you can't handle it, how can he or she be expected to handle it?

2. Don't make false promises. Do not promise anything that you are not absolutely sure of. If you don't know, say, "I don't know, but I will try to find out." Sweeping general promises such as "Everything will be all right" are particularly dangerous because they tend to minimize the seriousness of the event.

3. Don't make judgments about the young people with whom you're working. Be careful with your facial expressions, body language, inferences, and questions. The young person might interpret them to mean that he or she has done something wrong. The focus must be on the young person's needs at this time.

4. Don't play detective. Leave that to the people whose job it is and who are expected to do it. Instead, play the role of supporting the youth as they cope with the inevitable investigation.

5. Don't disrupt the structure of youths' lives more than necessary. Young people may complain about the burden of schoolwork, chores, or other responsibilities, but they need the structure of an ordinary day. Be sensible about expectations, and reduce the stress through

limiting time spent on any one task and through avoiding introduc-
ing new tasks or duties. This approach preserves a sense of security.

6. Don't withdraw from young people in emotional crisis. Other
    people may withdraw because they don't know what to do or say.
    Acknowledge privately to the young person that you know school-
    work or other chores may be difficult right now, but that you are
    willing to help him or her succeed. Then demonstrate that this is
    true.

The bottom line is that all people need to talk about their traumatic
experiences and integrate these experiences into their understanding of
themselves and of life in general. When people have the opportunity to
discuss, share, and compare experiences, the trauma loses its dominance
over their consciousness and begins to diffuse into their understanding of
themselves and their world.

The trauma never totally disappears. Adults often wish they could
make trauma vanish for children, but they cannot. When adults try to do
this for children, they increase the effect of the trauma because children
read the message that it is not OK to acknowledge that it is a part of
them forever.

Adapted from K. Johnson, *Trauma in the Lives of Children: Crisis and Stress Manage-
ment Techniques for Counselors and Other Professionals* (Alameda, Calif.: Hunter
House, 1989). Used by permission of Dr. Kay Schrader of the Indianapolis School Crisis
Response Team.

Common Behaviors of Children and Youth after a Crisis

Reminders for Parents and Other Adults Working with Children

Remember, these behaviors are normal after a crisis; the *event* is abnormal. After a crisis event, young people may:

1. Be irritable and grumpy about little things.

2. Be picky eaters or may eat everything in sight (teens may forget to eat).

3. Sleep poorly: have scary dreams, wake up often, be tired the next day.

4. Talk more than usual or be more silent than usual.

5. Be more emotional than usual. When a violent death has occurred, they may feel helpless or angry. Adults may need to caution them to express their anger in words and not act it out in ways they may regret later.

6. Fear both real and imagined things. Ghosts, burglars, bogeymen, monsters, and murderers may seem all alike to them.

7. Fear losing family members or friends. The younger the child, the more likely this fear will occur because younger children depend on others more for the basics of life.

Adults can help by:

1. Telling young people what happened and what is happening in words they can understand. This doesn't mean telling them all the gory details, but it does mean giving them correct information. If you don't know, tell them you don't know but that you will try to find out. Then do it.

2. Helping young people to talk about their thoughts and feelings about what happened by listening carefully and not putting them down for their thoughts or feelings. You don't have to agree with them. You can even say gently, "I can understand how you would think that, but I don't think it's that way. I think . . ." This intervention gives them another way to think about things without shutting off the communication.

3. Making allowances for grumpiness, unusual eating, or difficult sleep.

4. Accepting the fact that children will want to play about the event. This is how children accept emotionally difficult information. They may pretend to be dead to try to feel what it means to be dead because the concept is beyond their level of maturity. Some may act out violence. It is important for adults to stop dangerous behavior, help children understand the danger, and ask questions and listen to the answers so adults can shape what they learn.

5. Reassuring young people honestly about safety. Never say, "Everything will be OK." Everything isn't OK for them right now. Reassurance may come in words, but it may also include doing things differently at home to help everyone be more safe—new rules, locks and keys, different child-care arrangements. Some children need to know who will take care of them if their parent or guardian dies.

6. Letting teachers or other school people know what your child is coping with so they can be sensitive and helpful to the child.

The reactions listed above usually diminish significantly within a few weeks after the crisis event. Reactions to a suicide may last a little longer. When the event is a murder, it may take even longer for reactions to subside, especially if no suspect is in custody. Court cases that stretch over many months make it more difficult for people to put events behind them because current news coverage about developments in the case keep it fresh in the mind. When children (or adults) can understand that the criminal-justice system moves slowly to make sure that all the evidence supports a conviction of the right person, they are better able to move on with their lives.

When to Seek Professional Help

An evaluation by a mental-health professional is recommended if any of the following behavior is seen in a child or adolescent following a trauma:

1. Acts like absolutely nothing has happened after a crisis or serious loss. School work or work performance suffers or a young person fears going to school or work.

2. Hurts self intentionally or engages in high-risk behavior.

3. Talks about, threatens, or attempts suicide.

4. Panics frequently (has intense fear for no apparent reason).

5. Frequently physically assaults others or is cruel to animals.

6. Starts behaving poorly with family members.

7. Becomes involved with alcohol or drugs.

8. Begins committing delinquent acts.

9. Won't socialize with peers or starts to hang with "the wrong crowd."

Adapted from materials prepared for the Indianapolis School Crisis Response Team. Used by permission of Dr. Kay Schrader of the response team.

The suggestions on "When to Seek Professional Help" are adapted from Sister Teresa McIntier, "Signs that Bereavement in Children Needs Outside Intervention," from "Bereavement in Children," a workshop presented in Indianapolis by Carondelet Health Care of Tucson, Ariz., 1992.

Children, Youth, and Grief

I. Perceptions of Death

Maturity level affects how death is perceived. The ages below are approximations. Children and adults under the stress of grief often regress to earlier stages; adults, too, can fall into magical feeling or thinking when grieving even though they know the thought isn't realistic.

  A. The child at approximately ages three to five:
- Denies death as a final process.
- Sees death like sleep: You are dead, and then you are alive again. Or it is like a journey: Daddy goes to work, and then he comes home again.
- May think there is a magical solution: If I wish hard enough, Grandpa will come back.
- May connect unrelated events: Told that Uncle Harry died in his sleep, the child refuses to go to sleep. Overhearing that Grandma put her pajamas on, sat down in the chair, and died, the child refuses to wear pajamas.

  B. The child at approximately ages five to nine:
- Understands that death is final.
- Doesn't understand that it happens to all living things, especially self and caretakers.
- Retains much magical thinking. The child may fear that death is contagious or may assume that deaths are a result of burglars, ghosts, or bogeymen.

  C. The child at approximately ages nine to twelve:
- Recognizes that death is an inevitable experience.

- Realizes that even she or he will encounter death eventually.
- May still retain elements of magical thinking. The child may believe that death is a punishment. He may blame himself for not visiting the deceased. She may still believe that wishes can kill, even though she knows they can't. He may believe in one-to-one replacement—someone has to die so that someone else can be born.
- Has practical concerns about death: What happens to our family now that Grandpa is gone?

D. Teen-age youth:
   - Most understand death as universal, inevitable, and irreversible; some are still at earlier stages.
   - May see death as enemy of their changing bodies and say, "If you just grow up to die, What's the use?"
   - Need help in understanding their more adult-like emotions and help in learning how to act in the crisis.
   - May have childlike views of death (as may some adults). Such views commonly surface when we are in grief, but some individuals retain them throughout life, even when not grieving.
   - Adolescents and adults know that death is inevitable and final; yet their daily attitudes and actions may be more consistent with the belief that personal death is an unfounded rumor. Examples:
      - High-risk behaviors—smoking even though serious symptoms of lung deterioration have begun.
      - Unsafe sex though informed about dangers.
      - Refusing to drive sanely even after causing a serious crash.
      - Euphemistic language to talk about death—using such terms as sleeping, gone away, passed on, focusing on seeing the dead in the afterlife rather than on the fact of their absence in this life.

II.   Behaviors and Needs to Expect from Children and Youth in Grief
      The themes of grief recovery for children are the same as the themes for adults. What differs is the typical behaviors accompanying each theme and the needs of children for external support. These behaviors

and needs are related to the capability for understanding and the level of dependency.

A. Children of approximate ages three to five:
   1. Behaviors to expect:
      - Clingy, afraid of losing other family members.
      - May think "I did it."
      - May ask, "Hasn't he been dead enough?" or "When is he coming back?"
   2. Needs of the three- to five-year-old:
      - Kind, understanding tone of voice and demeanor. Often young children do not understand words and instead pick up feelings from nonverbal cues.
      - Encouragement to talk about how he feels in whatever way he can express it.
      - Permission to "play about" death and the events surrounding her experience.
      - Open, direct manner that says, "I'm with you and you are with me. There are no secrets."
      - Sharing of how you feel or felt when a similar thing happened.
      - Reassurance that remaining family members will take care of the child.

B. Children of approximate ages five to nine:
   1. Behaviors to expect:
      - Fear of ghosts, bogeymen, and anything or anyone associated with death, often including other children who are grieving.
      - Laughter or silly behavior to cover for their embarrassment at not knowing how to behave.
      - More sophisticated magical thinking may induce guilt if they think they have caused the death; they are more likely to be angry about the death than younger children.
      - May exhibit thinly veiled fear that other family members will die.
   2. Some common questions:
      - "How old are you, Mommy?" might mean "Are you going to die, too?"

- "Why are you taking that medicine?" might mean "Are you sick like Grandpa?"
- "Does Dad have cancer?" might mean "Is Dad going to die, too?" or maybe "Do all men die from cancer?"
  3. Needs of the five- to nine-year-old:
     - Clear answers in simple terms to the questions she asks, no matter how improbable her fears seem.
     - An accepting listener to the memories he has of the deceased.
     - Explanations to refute the magical beliefs that feed the fears.
     - Acceptance of play about the death, or artwork or songs about the events surrounding the death.
- C. Children of approximate ages nine to twelve:
  1. Behaviors to expect:
     - Attempts to be a grown-up—as he perceives a grown-up.
     - May clam up, isolate herself, and suppress feelings.
     - Many concerns about surface issues: "What do I say to Grandma?" "How should I act?" "I looked so stupid crying!" "Grandpa looked really gross!"
     - May cling to the bereaved silently.
     - May react with irritability or open rage.
  2. Needs of the nine- to twelve-year-old:
     - To be taken seriously, no matter how shallow her concerns seem.
     - To be included in family discussions about the changes brought about by the death.
     - To have his ways of grieving accepted.
     - For adults to understand that though the child understands death intellectually, there may be great difficulty in understanding it emotionally. Magical thinking may be pretty much gone, but magical feeling may persist.
- D. Teen-Age Years
  1. Behaviors to expect:
     - Wildly fluctuating emotional reactions—hysterical outbursts followed by embarrassed laughter.

- Idealization of the deceased followed by condemnation.
- Childish dependence or raging independence.
- Anger at anyone or anything available.
- Physical complaints—headaches, stomachaches.
- Expression of values inconsistent with those held previously.
- Extreme acting out—out-of-character behaviors, substance abuse, risky activities.

2. Needs of teenagers:
   - To be included in planning and decision-making.
   - To be informed of what to expect in terms of events, ceremonies, and rituals.
   - To know what to expect from various relatives.
   - To know what is expected of him or her.
   - To witness adults grieving so they can learn adult ways to grieve.
   - To be encouraged to talk about what they think and feel and have their thoughts and feelings respected.

Adapted from the resources cited below. Used by permission of Dr. Kay Schrader of the Indianapolis School Crisis Response Team.

Grollman, Earl A., ed. *Concerning Death: A Practical Guide for the Living.* Boston: Beacon Press, 1974.

Grollman, Earl A., ed. *Explaining Death to Children.* Boston: Beacon Press, 1967.

Schaefer, Dan, and Christine Lyons. *How Do We Tell the Children? Helping Children Understand and Cope when Someone Dies.* New York: Newmarket Press, 1988.

Do's and Don'ts for Talking with Young People about Death

Do's

1. Talk to young people about death before crisis strikes.
   a. None of us processes information very well when we are highly stressed.
   b. Remember that in this discussion, attitude may be more important than words. Talk in a quiet, honest, straightforward way that will encourage dialogue. Answer questions directly and listen closely.
   c. Adjust the information to the intellectual level and emotional capabilities of the child or adolescent.
   d. Present information in gradual stages according to the developmental level of the young person.

2. Encourage parents to involve children of all ages in the sorrow of the family.
   a. By supporting others through expressions of love, the young people gain a sense of their capability for helping others, and they feel less powerless.
   b. When young people are included in family sorrow as well as family joys, they truly feel that they belong.
   c. Young people can benefit from attending funerals if they want to attend, but they should be told what will happen so they know what to expect. If they do not want to attend the funeral, some other type of good-bye ceremony should be planned—lighting a candle, saying a prayer, or visiting the grave site.

3. Allow the young people to grieve in their own ways.
    a. Anger, tears, and protest are common reactions.
    b. Encourage young people to discuss their innermost fantasies, fears, and feelings. When these feelings are nonjudgmentally accepted by caring adults, young people can talk about them as often as necessary until the thoughts have less power.

4. Allow and encourage reminiscence about the lost person. Anger as well as affection must be permitted in the search for peace.

5. Read about, think about, and discuss your own thoughts and feelings about death. If you are disturbed by or feel uncomfortable talking about death, young people will sense this discomfort and pick up your attitudes

Don'ts

1. Don't try to protect young people from the sorrow surrounding death. "Mental health is not found in denial of tragedy but in frank acknowledgment of painful separation," writes Earl Grollman.

2. Never tell a child what she or he will later need to unlearn.
    a. Avoid fairy tales, half truths, circumlocutions—no long trips or journeys, being asleep, or in the hospital.
    b. Young people have enough trouble separating fantasy from reality without our confusing things further.

3. Avoid euphemisms.
    a. Use words like "dead," "stopped working," "wore out," "died."
    b. For suicide, use "committed suicide" or "killed himself" (or herself).
    c. For murder, use "murdered" or "was killed."
    d. Clearly tell young people some details of an accident so they don't hear it first from someone less sensitive to their feelings.
    e. Avoid equating death with sleep to prevent fear of going to sleep.

4. Don't talk about the deceased's sickness without explaining the difference between serious illnesses that people die from and the ordinary kinds of illnesses like colds, sore throats, and flu. Young people need the reassurance that they and their caretakers will not die from colds or the flu.

5. Be thoughtful about how you share your religious convictions.
    a. Avoid theological abstractions that confuse.
    b. Don't link suffering and death to God's punishment.
    c. Don't paint God as selfishly wanting or needing the deceased. Most children will resent such a God and fear that they or their caregivers may be taken away too.
    d. If heaven is where the deceased is said to be, be prepared for questions; look to the pastoral staff to assist you in this discussion.

Adapted from the resources cited below. Used by permission of Dr. Kay Schrader of the Indianapolis School Crisis Response Team.

Grollman, Earl A., ed. *Concerning Death: A Practical Guide for the Living.* Boston: Beacon Press, 1974.

Schaefer, Dan, and Christine Lyons. *How Do We Tell the Young People? Helping Young People Understand and Cope when Someone Dies.* New York: Newmarket Press, 1988.

Stories about Death
for Elementary School Children

(Grade levels in parentheses)

Adler, C.S. *Daddy's Climbing Tree*. New York: Clarion, 1993. Jessica
   refuses to believe the reality of her father's death when he is killed
   in a hit-and-run accident. A trip to the family's former home helps
   her to acknowledge the death and understand that she must adjust
   her way of thinking and living (3-6).

Aliki. *The Two of Them*. New York: Greenwillow Books, 1979. In short
   poems, this book tells of the love between a grandfather and his
   granddaughter, starting with her birth and ending with his death
   (K-3).

Bartoli, Jennifer. *Nonna*. New York: Harvey House, 1975. A boy nar-
   rates the story of his grandmother's death, including her funeral, the
   next day, and the first Christmas without her (3-6).

Boyd, Candy Dawson. *Circle of Gold*. New York: Scholastic, 1984.
   Mattie, an 11-year-old African-American girl, lives with her mother
   and brother. Everything in her life changes when her father is killed
   in a car accident. The book tells of the family's sorrow over the loss
   of a loved one and how they try to build a new life as a family
   (3-6).

Carrick, Carol. *The Accident*. New York: Seabury Press, 1976. A boy's
   dog is hit by a truck, and he deals with his anger and grief (1-3).

Clifton, Lucille. *Everett Anderson's Goodbye*. New York: Holt,
   Rinehart & Winston, 1983. A young African-American boy must
   deal with his father's death. His feelings are evoked in simple poems
   and are underscored in gentle pencil illustrations (K-3).

Cohn, Janice. *I Had a Friend Named Peter: Talking to Children about the Death of a Friend.* New York: Morrow, 1987. Betsy's best friend is killed by an automobile. This story tells how her parents and nursery school help Betsy to understand what happened (K-3).

De Paola, Tomie. *Nana Upstairs and Nana Downstairs.* New York: Putnam, 1973. A little boy must deal with the death of his great-grandmother (K-2).

Dragonwagon, Crescent. *Winter Holding Spring.* New York: Macmillan, 1990. After Sarah's mother dies, Sarah and her father spend time together helping each other to heal the hurt. The pattern of the book helps readers see the cycle of grieving that Sarah and her father weather (1-4).

Graeber, Charlotte Towner. *Mustard.* New York: Macmillan, 1982. Mustard is a cat with a heart ailment. His owner, eight-year-old Alex, has to live with Mustard's increasing infirmities and eventually cope with his death (K-3).

Greene, Constance C. *Beat the Turtle Drum.* New York: Viking, 1976. Katie, age 13, feels that "nothing will ever be right again" after her sister, age 11, is killed instantly in a fall from a tree. Katie's bereavement is expressed in simple but sensitive language (3-6).

Heegard, Marge Eaton. *Coping with Death and Grief.* Minneapolis: Lerner, 1990. Starting with a chapter about moving to a new city and progressing through the deaths of animals, friends, siblings, and various beloved family members, the book explains funerals, cremation, the different ways people die, and other details about which children are inquisitive (4-6).

Hesse, Karen. *Poppy's Chair.* New York: Macmillan, 1993. Leah is constantly reminded of her grandfather's absence on her first visit to her grandmother's house since his death. Her grandmother helps her to deal with her feelings of loss and fear. Together they remember the grandfather and comfort each other (K-2).

Johnson, Patricia P., and Donna R. Williams. *Morgan's Baby Sister.* San Jose, Calif.: Resource Publications, 1993. This is a read-aloud book for families who have experienced the death of a newborn (K-2).

Jukes, Mavis. *Blackberries in the Dark.* New York: Knopf, 1985. A boy spends the summer with his grandmother for the first time since his grandfather's death (3-5).

Juneau, Barbara F. *Sad but O.K.—My Daddy Died Today: A Child's View of Death*. Grass Valley, Calif.: Blue Dolphin, 1988. Told through the language of nine-year-old Kelly, the book details the dying of Kelly's father from a malignant brain tumor. The book describes every part of the sequence of the father's illness and eventual death (3-6).

Lee, Virginia. *The Magic Moth*. New York: Seabury Press, 1972. A family deals with the illness and death of their young middle child (2-3).

Mathis, Sharon Bell. *The Hundred Penny Box*. New York: Viking, 1975. A young boy spends time with his 100-year-old great-aunt through her weakening and death (2-4).

Miles, Miska. *Annie and the Old One*. Boston: Little, Brown, 1971. Annie tries to keep her Indian grandmother from finishing a rug, knowing she will die when it is done (1-4).

Paterson, Katherine. *The Bridge to Terabithia*. New York: HarperCollins, 1977. A boy tries to cope with the accidental death of his best friend (4-6).

Simon, Norma. *The Saddest Time*. Morton Grove, Ill.: Albert Whitman, 1986. Simon tells three stories in which people die and are mourned —an eight-year-old killed in an accident, a grandmother, and an uncle who dies after a long illness (K-2).

Smith, Doris Buchanan. *A Taste of Blackberries*. New York: Crowell, 1973. A boy sees his best friend die from a bee sting (3-4).

Stevens, Carla. *Stories from a Snowy Meadow*. New York: Seabury Press, 1976. The animals of the meadow hold memorial services and a funeral for their friend the vole when she dies (K-2).

Vigna, Judith. *Saying Goodbye to Daddy*. Morton Grove, Ill.: Albert Whitman, 1991. Clare deals with feelings of guilt, anger, denial, and grief after her father's death in a car accident (1-4).

Viorst, Judith. *The Tenth Good Thing about Barney*. New York: Atheneum, 1971. When a pet dies, his owner remembers all the good things about him (K-2).

Adapted from materials prepared for the Indianapolis School Crisis Response Team. Used by permission of Dr. Kay Schrader of the response team.

Coping with Grief: Books for Teens

Agee, James. *A Death in the Family*. New York: Bantam, 1989. Fiction. A Pulitzer Prize-winning novel appropriate for high-school students. Provides insight into how death affects a family, including the misunderstandings that often occur.

Angell, Judie. *Ronnie and Rosey*. Scarsdale, NY: Bradbury Press, 1977. Fiction. Ronnie's father is killed in a traffic accident on Halloween night. Ronnie and her mother must adjust to living in a new place and to a new life with just the two of them.

Blume, Judy. *Tiger Eyes*. Scarsdale, NY: Bradbury Press, 1981. Fiction. Davey's father is murdered in a robbery at his convenience store, and Davey must cope with the death. A realistic tale of some of the possible consequences of a violent death.

Bunting, Eve. *Face at the Edge of the World*. New York: Clarion Books, 1988. Fiction. Seventeen-year-old Jed is a bright, sensitive young man. But he must contend with problems that would overwhelm a mature adult. His best friend, Charlie, has just committed suicide, Jed's mother died when she gave birth to him, and his father blames him for her death. Jed uses his powers of observation and his love for his friend to uncover the answer to why Charlie killed himself.

Burnett, Frances Hodgson. *The Secret Garden*. New York: Lippincott, 1962. Fiction. Story of a young girl, orphaned and with multiple losses, and how she and others heal through friendship and nature.

Carter, Forrest. *The Education of Little Tree*. Albuquerque, N. Mex.: University of New Mexico Press, 1986. Nonfiction. A story of a Cherokee boyhood of the 1930s, detailing poignant, heartfelt losses, encouraging grandparents, and the rich language and beauty of nature.

Cleaver, Vera. *Where the Lilies Bloom.* Philadelphia: Lippincott-Raven, 1969. Fiction. The death of the father means the children will become orphans and wards of the state.

Cleaver, Vera, and Bill Cleaver. *Grover.* Philadelphia: Lippincott, 1970. Fiction. A mother, terminally ill with cancer, decides she does not want her family to watch her suffer through a long illness. She commits suicide, and her son and husband are faced with having to put their lives back together.

Craven, Margaret. *I Heard the Owl Call My Name.* New York: Dell, 1973. Fiction. A young priest learns from the Alaskan Indians he serves how to regard his own life and death.

Farley, Carol. *The Garden Is Doing Fine.* New York: Atheneum, 1975. Fiction. Corrie, a high-school freshman, has the same wishes and dreams as her best friend, but Corrie's father is in a hospital dying. Corrie eventually realizes that her father will die, but that he also will live on through the memories of those who knew him.

Frank, Anne. *Anne Frank: The Diary of a Young Girl.* Bantam, 1993. Nonfiction. The diary of a young teen in hiding from the Nazis in Europe. Depicts the many losses associated with war.

Gravelle, Karen, and Charles Haskins. *Teenagers Face to Face with Bereavement.* New York: Basic Books, 1989. Nonfiction. A group of teens in a grief support group wrote this book with their leader, each telling his or her story of grief and reconciliation. Offers hope that grieving people can feel better with time.

Grollman, Earl A. *Straight Talk about Death for Teenagers: How to Cope with Losing Someone You Love.* Boston: Beacon Press, 1993. Nonfiction. A "write-in" book with thought-starters in the form of poems, notes, feelings, snippets of useful information. Unique format to encourage teens to put their ideas and feelings into words.

Gunther, John. *Death Be Not Proud.* New York: Harper & Row, 1971. Nonfiction. Chronicles a courageous teenager's decline and death from a brain tumor. Appropriate for middle- and high-school students.

Hughes, Monica. *Hunter in the Dark.* Avon, 1984. Fiction. This Canadian book tells the story of a successful 17-year-old, Mike, who suddenly becomes seriously ill. The illness turns out to be leukemia, and Mike's parents decide to keep the truth from him. We see how Mike discovers the truth and how he learns to cope with the attendant implications of the illness.

Hunter, Mollie. *A Sound of Chariots*. New York: Harper & Row, 1972.
Fiction. The story covers the life of Birdie, a girl growing up in
Scotland after World War I, from the death of her father when she is
eight until she is 18 and finally able to sort out most of her feelings
about her father's death.

Huntsberry, W.E. *The Big Hangup*. New York: Lathrop, 1970. Fiction.
Teens deal with their grief and guilt after a friend dies in an auto
accident involving teen drinking and driving. Starkly realistic, this
story shows the guilt and self-blame that many teens feel after a
tragic accident.

Jury, M., and. D. Jury. *Gramps*. New York: Penguin Books, 1978.
Nonfiction. One family's encounter with the reality of a grandfather's death. Rural setting, photos tell the story. Both old and
young experience the losses of aging.

Kidd, R. *That's What Friends Are For*. Nashville, Tenn.: Thomas
Nelson, Inc., 1978. Fiction. Two inseparable 13-year-old friends
confront death when one of them is diagnosed with leukemia.

Kolehmainen, Janet, and Sandra Handwerk. *Teen Suicide: A Book for
Friends, Family, and Classmates*. Minneapolis: Lerner, 1986.
Nonfiction. An easy-to-read book for survivors and those who may
know a potentially suicidal teen. The authors use fictionalized
vignettes from the lives of hurting teens to illustrate the facts and
myths of suicide.

Krementz, Jill. *How It Feels When a Parent Die*s. New York: Alfred A.
Knopf, 1983. Nonfiction. Reassurance that all the feelings that
accompany the grief following a parent's death are normal.

Lewis, Oscar. *Death in the Sanchez Family*. New York: Random House,
1970. Nonfiction. Written from interviews with a poor Mexican
family, the story shows the family's dignity and cultural continuity
in the face of death. Brings to awareness the many losses and struggles of the poor.

Lund, Doris. *Eric*. New York: Dell, 1974. Nonfiction. How Eric lives to
the fullest before he dies, described by his mother. Appropriate for
middle school and up.

Mann, Peggy. *There Are Two Kinds of Terrible*. New York: Doubleday,
1977. Fiction. Robbie breaks his arm on the last day of school and
has to spend his whole summer vacation in a cast. That is one kind
of terrible. But he finds out about another kind of terrible when his

mother goes into the hospital for tests and never returns. He is left with a father he barely knows and without his mother, the person he loved most in the world.

Martin, Ann M. *With You and Without You*. New York: Scholastic, 1986. Fiction. Liza's father has been told that he will die in the next six months. The entire family responds by vowing to make his last days memorable and pleasurable. When he dies, each family member responds differently to the loss. Liza feels angry and guilty and cannot understand why others are not mourning their loss. Eventually she realizes that all grieve in their own way and that she indeed must go on with her life.

Morris, Jeannie. *Brian Piccolo: A Short Season*. Rand McNally, 1971. Nonfiction. Portrays the life of a successful professional athlete who dies after a seven-month battle with cancer. Includes issues of racism and its associated losses. Appropriate for middle school and up.

Paterson, Katherine. *Bridge to Terabithia*. New York: HarperCollins, 1977. Fiction. The story of the friendship of ten-year-old Jess and his close friend, Leslie. Together they create the secret kingdom of Terabithia. Leslie is killed and Jess must deal with her death. Their Terabithia enables him to cope. Appropriate for intermediate grades and up.

Peck, Richard. *Father Figure*. New York: Viking, 1988. Fiction. Byron and Jim's mother takes her own life when she can no longer tolerate her cancer. The boys and their mother had been living with their grandmother, who now finds she cannot deal with her grief and the boys' needs. She sends them to their estranged father. The story tells how Jim finally lets go of his rage at his father's desertion, his mother's death, and his grandmother's aloof and controlling behavior.

Richter, Elizabeth. *Losing Someone You Love: When a Brother or Sister Dies*. New York: Putnam, 1986. Nonfiction. Young people ages 10 to 24 discuss candidly their experiences following the death of a sibling.

Rofes, Eric E., ed. *The Kid's Book about Death and Dying*. Boston: Little, Brown, & Co., 1985. Nonfiction. Students ages 11 to 14 explore their feelings and thoughts about death and grief, ranging from causes of death, euthanasia, and funerals to graveyards.

Shreve, Susan Richards. *Family Secrets: Five Very Important Stories*. New York: Alfred A. Knopf, 1979. Fiction. Three of these stories deal with death: a family dog dies, a terminally ill grandmother comes to live with the family, and the teen-age brother of a best friend commits suicide.

Thesman, Jean. *The Last April Dancers*. Boston: Houghton Mifflin, 1987. Fiction. Cat's 16th birthday is marked by ecstasy and agony. She receives beautiful and exciting gifts, spends most of the day with Cameron, the young man she loves, and earns her driver's license. But this is the day that she lets her father know how angry she is at home, and this is the day her father commits suicide. The book deals with many concerns of adolescents, including Cat's feelings of guilt over believing that she has killed her father.

Zindel, Paul. *Pardon Me, You're Stepping on My Eyeball!* New York: Harper & Row, 1976. Fiction. A true-to-life story about teens living in less-than-ideal families encountering death.

Zindel, Paul. *The Pigman*. New York: Harper & Row, 1968. Fiction. Realistic story popular with young teens with death as a recurring theme.

Adapted from materials prepared for the Indianapolis School Crisis Response Team. Used by permission of Dr. Kay Schrader of the crisis team.

An Interim Pastor's First Sunday Sermon

The God Who Won't Let Go

This sermon was preached by the Rev. Ronald W. Smith on his first Sunday as transitional pastor of Northminster Presbyterian Church, Indianapolis.

Text: Romans 8:28-39

You might think that after such a long time it would be easy. But there are still occasions that find me groping for how to say what is in my heart. One such occasion is saying "Good-bye," as I did last Sunday after ten years in Rochester, Minnesota. And then again today, as I come to say "Hello" to you.

This is not an ordinary day for any of us. It is a day of change. It is a day that many of you have looked forward to with a mixture of anticipation and dread. Anticipation, because you want the congregation to set a course for the future and move forward. Dread, because it is another step in the realization that Dr. and Mrs. Mathias are gone—that the Mathias era at Northminster has ended.

For me it is more than a change of congregations. I have never been a "transitional pastor" before. It is, in fact, a new idea that was designed for this congregation at this particular time. I understand that my job is to help pull things together and make sure that we are doing the best we can in Christian nurture, in pastoral care of members, in outreach and evangelism, in taking care of these buildings and grounds. It is my job to work with the other members of the staff to design and lead worship that will be honor the Lord and touch our hearts. It is my job to preach sermons that will help the congregation to grow in faith and commitment. And, it will be my job, starting sometime next year, to work with you through a comprehensive evaluation of the congregation's strengths and opportunities, and to begin establishing long-range goals for Northminster's ministry to the city of Indianapolis.

But, before any of those things, I will listen to the things that are in your hearts so that I can help you practice good stewardship of the pain you have experienced in the murder of your pastor and his wife. Many of you have felt as if you were somehow victims of this crime yourselves —the assault that took their lives also took something from you.

But you have already starting moving beyond this feeling of victimization—some have moved further than others. The question for us as a Christian people is always, "How can we offer up the experience of our lives as an offering to God?" How can we practice good Christian stewardship of all the things we experience—the evil as well as the good? We have an example before us in Jesus Christ, who suffered the pain and humiliation of crucifixion. Yet, because he offered those horrible experiences to God, his death has become a door to life for all the world.

Last year Cardinal [Joseph] Bernardin of Chicago died of cancer. He had chosen to disclose his terminal illness several months earlier so that he could bear witness to the faithfulness of Christ in his dying as he had borne witness to him in his life. Through his witness, Cardinal Bernardin gave courage and hope to countless people. Fred and Cleta Mathias did not have an opportunity to bear such a witness, though we have no doubt they would have done so if it had been possible. The murderer's crime silenced their voices, but it must not be permitted to silence the faith by which they lived. And so my first and greatest responsibility as your pastor will be to help give you a voice to bear witness, a voice that will well up out of the tragedy as a great song of faith to all those around us who need a faith to live by. It will be my task to join hands and arms with you so that together we may demonstrate the surpassing love of God to people all around us who need to find the love that will never let them go. Together, we will unwrap the wounds of our hearts so that people all around us—wounded and hurting people—will see and know that they can come to Northminster Church with their broken hearts and needy lives and they will be welcomed here in Christ's name.

So, this is no ordinary day for you or for me. It is the beginning of a time of transition and change for us all. Though my ministry with you is of limited duration, we will not be merely marking time. It will be a time of active engagement in ministry and mission, of exploring the possibilities for the future and setting a course toward those possibilities as God gives us direction. Where do we begin?

We begin by going back to the foundation stones upon which are built all that we are and all we hope to do in Christ's name. I can think of no better place to begin than at this table of Holy Communion and with the words we have heard from St. Paul's letter to the church in Rome. The section from which our lesson comes begins at verse 18 with these words: "I consider that the sufferings of this present time are not worth comparing with the glory about to be revealed to us." This is a mighty strong statement in the face of all that was happening to the Roman Christians, and it is still a strong statement in the face of what has happened here. Then, in the climactic verses of this magnificent chapter, the Apostle spells out the reason for his boldness. We can perhaps best understand what Paul is saying if we hear these verses as answers to three great questions that arise from the experience of suffering and death.

The first great question is this: Is God for us or against us? We go along living in the sunshine of a happy life and then, one day, something happens to us or to someone we love—a car accident, financial ruin, a divorce, or even murder. And suddenly we find ourselves asking, "How can something like this happen? Is God for us or against us? Is there, deep at the center of reality, a loving heart? Or are we orphans in the universe with no heavenly father to watch over us? Does God care what happens to us, or do our lives and deaths mean nothing at all?" The answer of faith is clear and unmistakable. We do matter to God. God is for us. Yes, grief and trouble will come our way, as it does to all people—there is no exemption from suffering. Cancer will strike the best as well as the worst. The devout will have a full measure of life's pain. Oh how we wish it were different. Like Billy Pilgrim in Kurt Vonnegut's book *Slaughterhouse Five,* we want a life in which everything is beautiful and nothing hurts. But it will not be that way. Still, with the Apostle we can say, "God is for us!" And not just for us, but for all people. Upon what does he base this affirmation? Where do we turn for the evidence of God's care? We turn to Jesus—God's beloved Son—who was not spared the humiliation and pain of the cross, but was given up for us all. Yes, when life puts the question about God's love, we turn to Jesus and find the answer in him.

The second question that arises from our human condition concerns the possibility that we have somehow lost God's love because of our failure and sin. We may say, "Yes, yes. God loved me once upon a time when I was pure and innocent. But now . . . ?" Is it possible that God might turn away from us in disgust because we have not lived as we should? I have heard of parents disowning a son or a daughter because of some terrible misdeed. A child slips into a life of debauchery, and the father says, "He is no longer my child!" Is it possible that the suffering we experience is because in a moment of terrible anger God turned away? No! Listen again: "Who will bring any charge against God's elect? God has declared us free from sin." The only one in heaven or on the earth who has the right to judge is Jesus Christ. And what does the Scripture say of his judgment? "It is the Judge who died for us, who was raised for us, who sits at the right hand of God and intercedes for us." No, we cannot lose God's love. We may waver in our love for God, but God never wavers in his love for us.

The third question that arises from our human situation concerns the possibility of some ultimate separation from God. We know that in this world all things must end. Loss and separation are an inevitable part of everyone's experience. A husband and wife may live together for 30, 40, 50 years or more. But finally they will be separated by death. Is that the last word? Does death have the final say? We must answer, "No!" Why? Because with the Apostle we have been given grace to believe that "neither death, nor life, nor angels, nor rulers, nor powers, nor height, nor depth, nor anything else in all creation, will be able to separate us from the love of God in Christ Jesus our Lord."

As a young minister in my first church out of seminary, I went through the agonizing experience of almost losing my faith in God. For a variety of reasons that I need not go into here I had come to question everything. I remember sitting in my study one day in great inward distress because I was so full of doubts. I had tried to pray my way through —but the questions would not be silent. On that day I resolved to go back to the foundation stones of faith and see what was left for me to believe in. After long meditation on this question I decided that I did believe there must be some kind of power behind the created order of

the universe. I also believed that, though the evidence was highly am-
biguous, it was likely that this power was benevolent. I wasn't sure what
Jesus had to do with all of this, except that I could not say the name of
Jesus without tears welling up in my eyes.

Not long after that day in the study I went to Miami, Florida, to a
national convention of the Southern Baptist churches. I attended a few
of the meetings, but mostly I sat in a dark hotel room and thought about
my loss of faith and what I should do about it. I also spent time in the
hotel bar drinking rum and Coke. Let me tell you, the mixture of alcohol and doubt is a very potent recipe for depression.

Before the convention I had received an invitation to dinner at one
of the swanky hotels on Miami Beach. For some reason I decided to
attend. When I arrived I found that I was one of a small group of 40 to
50 young Baptist preachers who had been identified by somebody as
"rising stars" in the church. There were three speakers—a movie star, a
professional football player, and a world-class nuclear physicist named
Edward Schwitzer. The movie star and the football player told their
stories. It was the usual kind of pep talk and inspirational message.

When it came Schwitzer's turn, however, there was a surprise in
store. Dr. Schwitzer spoke for about 15 minutes to a room that sat in
shocked silence. He spoke of the church's failure and hypocrisy. It was
1966. You know what was going on in this country—civil rights, the war
on poverty, Vietnam, uprisings on college campuses. Schwitzer spoke
about the terrible silence of the church on these critical issues. He spoke
about the long legacy of racism that was still alive in too many congregations. And then, as if to me, he spoke about the need for breathing
room in the church. He asked if it were possible for a person of intellectual honesty to survive in a church that allowed no room for diversity.
He closed with a stinging rebuke of the denomination's leaders and a
question concerning whether or not it was possible for the church to be
saved.

When the moderator was handed the microphone, he said, "Well,
Dr. Schwitzer, you have certainly given us something to think about. It
is important to note that you have not left the church." At that point Dr.
Schwitzer took the microphone back and said, "Not yet!"

And then he continued, and his words were as fresh water to my
parched soul. He said, "I'll tell you why I have not left the church. It is
because Jesus Christ has taken hold of me and won't let go." I looked

down as tears filled my eyes and dropped into my plate. I knew that I had touched bedrock in those words of Edward Schwitzer. "Jesus Christ has taken hold of me and he won't let go."

My new friends . . . my soon-to-be friends . . . this is the bedrock on which we can stand as we start this new time together. If the future of the church depended on our ability to hold on to God, then we would be in deep trouble. But it is not our hold on God that matters so much as God's hold on us. And ours is a God who will not let us go.

Proclaimed for the people of God
at Northminster Presbyterian Church
June 1, 1997
Ronald W. Smith

Reprinted by permission of Ronald W. Smith.

Chapter One

1. Herbert Anderson and Kenneth R. Mitchell, *All Our Losses, All Our Griefs* (Philadelphia: Westminster Press, 1983), 137.

2. Anne Sutherland, "Worldframes and God-talk in Trauma and Suffering," *The Journal of Pastoral Care* 49, no. 3 (1995), 280.

3. Ibid., 280.

4. J. Timothy Allen, "God-talk and Myth: Turning Chaos into Comfort," *The Journal of Pastoral Care* 46, no. 4 (1992), 340.

5. Anderson and Mitchell, *All Our Losses*, 171.

6. Harold S. Kushner, *When Bad Things Happen to Good People* (New York: Schocken Books, 1981), 138.

7. Brian Horne, *Imagining Evil* (London: Darton, Longman and Todd, Ltd., 1996), 21.

8. Allan Janssen, "The Problem of Evil," *Basic Beliefs* Unit I: God in the World, Adult Foundational Curriculum (Louisville, Ky.: Presbyterian Publishing House, 1996), 7.

9. Kushner, *When Bad Things Happen to Good People*, 142.

10. Warren W. Wiersbe, *When Bad Things Happen to God's People* (Old Tappan, N.J.: Fleming Revell Co., 1984), 126.

11. Ibid., 115.

12. Ibid., 84-86.

13. Ibid., 123.

14. Janssen, "The Problem of Evil," 8.

15. Andrew Delbanco, *The Death of Satan—How Americans Have Lost the Sense of Evil* (New York: Farrar, Straus & Giroux, 1995), 234.

16. Anderson and Mitchell, *All Our Losses*, 172.

17. Delbanco, *The Death of Satan*, 235.

18. Burton Z. Cooper, *Why God?* (Atlanta: John Knox Press, 1988), 34.

19. Ibid.

20. Ibid., 123.

21. Anderson and Mitchell, *All Our Losses*, 171.

22. Paul Tillich, "The Eternal Now," in Herman Feifel, *The Meaning of Death* (New York: McGraw-Hill, 1959), 35-36.

23. Marjorie J. Thompson, "Moving Toward Forgiveness," *Weavings: A Journal of the Christian Spiritual Life* 7, no. 2 (Nashville: Upper Room, April-May 1992), 16.

24. William Klassen, *The Forgiving Community* (Philadelphia: Westminster Press, 1966), 11.

25. Kushner, *When Bad Things Happen to Good People*, 148.

Chapter Two

1. C. A. Frolkey, "Critical Incidents and Traumatic Events: The Difference," *The Employee Assistance Program Digest*, 1992.

2. Andrew J. Weaver, *Psychological Trauma: What Clergy Need to Know* (n.p.: Human Sciences Press, Inc.), 385.

3. Linda Austin, *Responding to Disaster—A Guide for Mental Health Professionals* (Los Angeles: American Psychiatric Press, 1992), 61.

4. Ibid., 4.

5. Michael J. Scott and Stephen G. Stradling, *Counseling for Post-Traumatic Stress Disorder* (London: Sage Publications, 1992), 86.

6. S. Epstein, "The Self Concept, the Traumatic Neuroses and the Structure of Personality," in *Perspectives on Personality* 3 (Greenwich, Conn.: JAI Press, 1990), 26.

7. David W. Foy, ed., *Treating Post-Traumatic Stress Disorder: Cognitive-Behavorial Strategies* (New York: Guilford Press, 1992), 10.

8. Weaver, *Psychological Trauma*, 386.

9. K. Johnson, *Trauma in the Lives of Children: Crisis and Stress Management for Counselors and Other Professionals* (Alameda, Calif.: Hunter House, 1989).

10. Grady Bray and Jeff Mitchell, *Emergency Services Stress:*

Guidelines for Preserving the Health and Careers of Emergency Services Personnel (Englewood Cliffs, N.J.: Prentice Hall, Career & Technology, 1990), 31.

11. Lula Redmond, *Surviving: When Someone You Love Was Murdered—A Professional's Guide to Group Grief Therapy for Families and Friends of Murder Victims* (Clearwater, Fla.: Psychological Consultation & Education Services, Inc., 1989), 10.

12. Kay Schrader, workshop packet for St. Vincent Crisis Response Team.

13. Anderson and Mitchell, *All Our Losses*, 30.

14. Judith Kolf, *When Will I Stop Hurting?* (Grand Rapids: Baker Book House, 1987), 12.

15. Ibid., 36.

16. Ibid., 42.

17. D. O'Toole, *Bridging the Bereavement Gap: A Comprehensive Manual for the Programming of Hospice Bereavement Services* (Burnsville, N.C.: published by author, 1986).

18. Peter Steinke, *Healthy Congregations* (Bethesda, Md.: Alban Institute, 1996), 30.

19. Anderson and Mitchell, *All Our Losses*, 192.

Chapter Four

1. United Methodist Committee on Relief, *United Methodist Committee on Relief Training Manual* (New York: General Board of Global Ministries of the United Methodist Church, n.d.), 3.

2. Ibid., 20.

Chapter Five

1. A beautiful book that includes writing and examples of the art from the conference is available for $20 plus postage from The Oklahoma Arts Institute, P.O. Box 18154, Oklahoma City, OK 73154. Orders may be faxed to (405) 848-4538. The book was made possible through a grant from Southwestern Bell.

2. I am grateful to Kay Schrader of the St. Vincent Crisis Response

Team, who also coordinates the Indianapolis School Crisis Response Team, for permission to print the bibliographies in appendixes F and G.

Chapter Six

1. Carol McDonald, "A Congregation in Trauma: Reflection on the Worship Life of Northminster Presbyterian Church in Indianapolis, Indiana," unpublished paper delivered as a sabbatical report, March 1997.

2. Anderson and Mitchell, *All Our Losses*, 141.

3. Ibid.,140.

4. Ronald Smith, "The God Who Won't Let Go," a sermon delivered to Northminster Presbyterian Church, Indianapolis, Indiana, on June 1, 1997. See appendix H.

5. Carol McDonald, "A Congregation in Trauma."

6. John L. Bell and Graham Maule, *When Grief Is Raw: Songs for Times of Sorrow and Bereavement* (Scotland: Iona Community, 1997), 4. Available in the United States at $7.95 plus postage and handling from GIA Publications, Inc., 7404 S. Mason Avenue, Chicago, IL 60638. GIA's toll-free number is (800) GIA-1358.

7. Walter Brueggeman, "Foreword," in Ann Weems, *Psalms of Lament* (Louisville, Ky.: Westminster John Knox Press, 1995), x-xi.

8. Bell and Maule, *When Grief Is Raw*, 5.

9. Weems, *Psalms of Lament*, xvi.

Chapter Seven

1. *The Indianapolis Star*, Indianapolis, Ind., February 16, 1997, A01.

2. *The Indianapolis Star,* March 2, 1997, A01.

3. Redmond, *Surviving:*, 53.

4. *The Indianapolis Star*, June 15, 1997, A01.

5. Vera K. White, *A Call to Hope: Living as Christians in a Violent Society* (New York: Friendship Press, 1997), 56.

6. Redmond, *Surviving*, 4.

7. I am grateful to Judith Cebula, religion writer at *The Indianapolis Star*, for assistance in writing this section of the book.

8. Judith Cebula, interview with the author, August 12, 1997.

9. Austin, *Responding to Disaster*, 134.

10. National Victim Center, "Crime Victims' Privacy Rights in the Media" (Arlington, Va.: [National Victim Center], 1997), available at www.nvc.org.

11. Austin, introduction to *Responding to Disaster*. Austin's statistics are from the 1989 *Broadcasting and Cable Yearbook*.

12. Rich Van Wyck, interview with the author, August 12, 1997.

13. Redmond, *Surviving*, 38.

14. National Victim Center, "Overview of the Criminal Justice System" (Arlington, Va. [National Victim Center], 1977), available at www.nvc.org.

15. Ibid.

16. Redmond, *Surviving*, 62.

17. Anne Delaplane and David Delaplane, *Victims: A Manual for Clergy and Congregations*, 5th ed. (Denver: Spiritual Dimension in Victim Services, n.d.), 180. Available through The Spiritual Dimension in Victim Services, P.O. Box 6736, Denver, CO 80206-0736.

18. John Russo, "Retribution or Restoration?," unpublished paper, May 1997.

Chapter Eight

1. Grace Lindsay and J.D. Lindsay, "The Recovery Environment: Continuing Stressor vs. a Healing Psychological Space," in B.J. Sowder and M. Lystad, eds., *Disasters and Mental Health: Contemporary Perspectives and Innovations in Services to Disaster Victims* (Washington: American Psychiatric Press, 1986), 137-40.

2. Austin, *Responding to Disaster*, 61.

Chapter Nine

1. Charles M. Olsen, "A Structure for Congregational Stories," unpublished copyrighted paper, 1997, 1.

2. Mary Susan Gast, "Hope in the Strongholds of Violence," *Courage in the Struggle for Justice and Peace*, United Church of

Christ 9, no. 8 (Dec/Jan 1994-95), 4. (The publication is a UCC curriculum resource.)

3. Fay Angus, *How to Do Everything Right and Live to Regret It* (New York: Harper & Row, 1983), 160.